PSYCHOLOGY LIBRARY EDITIONS: MEMORY

Volume 11

ORGANISATION AND MEMORY

ORGANISATION AND MEMORY

A review, and a project in subnormality

PETER HERRIOT, JOSEPHINE M. GREEN AND
ROY MCCONKEY

Psychology Press
Taylor & Francis Group
LONDON AND NEW YORK

First published in 1973

This edition first published in 2014
by Psychology Press
27 Church Road, Hove, East Sussex BN3 2FA, UK

and by Psychology Press
711 Third Avenue, New York, NY 10017

Psychology Press is an imprint of the Taylor and Francis Group, an informa business

First issued in paperback 2015

British Library Cataloguing in Publication Data
A catalogue record for this book is available from the British Library

ISBN 978-1-84872-321-4 (Set)
eISBN 978-1-315-77503-6 (Set)
ISBN 978-1-84872-360-3 (hbk) (Volume 11)
ISBN 978-1-138-97767-9 (pbk) (Volume 11)
ISBN 978-1-315-79575-1 (ebk) (Volume 11)

Publisher's Note
The publisher has gone to great lengths to ensure the quality of this book but points out that some imperfections from the original may be apparent.

Disclaimer
The publisher has made every effort to trace copyright holders and would welcome correspondence from those they have been unable to trace.

Methuen Studies in Mental Handicap

Editor: Peter Mittler

Organisation and Memory

A review, and a project in subnormality

Peter Herriot,
Josephine M. Green,
Roy McConkey

Methuen & Co. Ltd.

London

First published in 1973
by Methuen & Co Ltd,
11 New Fetter Lane,
London EC4

SBN 416 77590 X

Setting by Tek-Art, London SE25
Printed in Great Britain
by Whitstable Litho, Straker Brothers Ltd

Contents

FIGURES AND TABLES

Preface

This book is intended to be primarily an account of a research project consisting of a series of related experiments using subnormal subjects. It is written for psychologists engaged in research in subnormality and those concerned with the experimental psychology of memory. The first section of the book, concerning organisation of memory in normals, is longer than might be expected in order to familiarise researchers in subnormality with the basic concepts and findings in the area. This review might also be useful to students of experimental psychology. The account of research which occupies most of the second section is arranged in logical rather than chronological order. It does not aim to provide an exhaustive account of findings so much as a selective interpretation.

The authors would like to thank their colleagues at the Hester Adrian Research Centre for their stimulating discussion; Alyce Sandes for typing the several manuscripts and Judith Wilding for help with the tables; the medical officers, supervisors, staff and trainees of the Adult Training Centres and the teachers and children of the Special Schools in the Manchester Area for helping in the experiments; Micky Cox, Kath Fraser, Christopher Wells, and Margaret Bates for their assistance in the carrying out of three of the experiments; and Methuen for their continued support.

Most of the research was carried out while the senior author (P.H.) was in receipt of a grant from the Leverhulme Trust, and while another author (R.Mc.) was in receipt of a Northern Ireland Postgraduate Studentship.

Editorial Foreword

Peter Mittler

After decades of neglect, mentally handicapped people are at last receiving a greater measure of public and professional concern. Responsibility for the education of children has now passed from the health to the education authorities; conditions in long stay hospitals are beginning to improve now that greater financial resources and more effective planning are being introduced, and more determined attempts are being made not only to prevent unnecessary admission to hospitals but to provide comprehensive services in the community.

These improvements are only just beginning, and a great deal remains to be done. It is not enough to erect buildings, provide services, spend money, or even recruit staff without also thinking about what is going to happen inside the buildings, what the staff of the new services are going to do and how mentally handicapped people will actually benefit. Not enough thought has yet been given to our aims and objectives in helping handicapped people, and to the ways in which these might be attained. It may not be enough to proclaim that we wish to help each person 'to develop to the best of his ability and to realise his full potential' if we cannot adequately define ability, or no longer believe in the idea of potential. We shall probably have to revise many ideas and assumptions which have guided us in the past, and begin to develop more effective ways of working with handicapped people, and of helping them to work with us.

Research has an important part to play in this task. In focusing on a specific problem, the research worker is forced to define, identify and isolate the variables which he wishes to examine; he may start from theory but he has to deal objectively with facts and data. He has to think clearly about the problem he has set himself, and to decide whether it lends itself to testable hypotheses and empirical study.

But research need not be conducted in isolation. It thrives best in the context of practical situations, and should be informed by a spirit of enquiry which is not confined to the research worker alone. Indeed, it might be argued that research is too important to be left to the research worker. His task is incomplete if he has failed to communicate not merely to his fellow specialists but to other practitioners such as teachers, nurses, social workers and parents. Moreover, communication here involves much more than informing others about his research findings. It includes helping others to adopt a research attitude to the problems which confront them. Teachers, for example, are apt to think of research workers as a race apart, descending from time to time from their ivory towers to collect their information and then disappearing for indefinite periods to commune with computers. This stereotype is not entirely groundless but there are hopeful signs of change.

It is important to realise that research can take many forms, and serve a variety of purposes. It cannot be judged purely by the extent to which it solves practical problems. Some projects will always need to be of a basic or fundamental nature, and may therefore strike the impatient practitioner as irrelevant to the 'real world'. The distinction between basic and applied research is far from clear cut; it is more useful to see them as lying on a continuum. A project may need to begin in the 'laboratory', leaning heavily on models, theories and techniques derived from experimental psychology. It can then develop in a more applied direction without sacrifice of rigour or objectivity by applying or translating research findings in the classroom, the hospital ward or in the home situation. Other research projects can be put to practical use much more quickly.

This series of 'Studies in Mental Handicap' is designed to provide accounts of a wide variety of projects. Some will inevitably be more specialised than others, and the readership of each volume in the series will not necessarily be the same. The series will exemplify a range of research strategies and research content, though the emphasis in most of them will be educational and psychological.

The present volume and others already planned constitute reports of work carried out at the Hester Adrian Research Centre, University of Manchester. The Centre was established in 1968 and now consists of about twenty full-time research staff, mostly working in small teams consisting of two or three people. Projects at present in progress or about to begin are concerned with language and communication skills; attentional aspects of learning; sign-reading by SSN children; visual perceptual skills and programmed instruction; evaluation and development of habilitation services provided in Adult Training Centres; the use of behaviour modification techniques in teaching hyperkinetic and non-ambulant profoundly retarded children; the development of visually directed reaching in Down's Syndrome infants; parental involvement in facilitating the development of young children; motivational aspects of transfer of learning; characteristics of severely ESN children in the North West.

The present volume by Dr Herriot, Mrs Green and Mr McConkey is concerned with memory – a topic which is of central importance to both teachers and psychologists, but which they tend to approach from somewhat different points of view. The work takes as its point of departure the substantial body of research which has been conducted by experimental psychologists on normal subjects. It deals with the nature of the processes which people use to try to impose some degree of organisation on incoming material which has to be remembered. It asks whether subnormal individuals differ from normals in respect of these processes, whether the differences can be regarded as quantitative or qualitative, and whether subnormal people can be helped by changing the ways in which the material is presented or has to be recalled. In other words, the authors are not content, as others have been, merely to demonstrate that subnormals have specific difficulties in certain kinds of task: they proceed to investigate the conditions under which they might be helped to improve their performance. This book illustrates one aspect of the relationship between theory and practice. Other volumes in the series will examine the same complex relationship from different perspectives.

Part One

Organisation and memory in the normal

Chapter 1

The process model of memory

a. *Memory processes*

The term memory is often used of behaviour in everyday life which requires a person to pay attention to something and later to recall it; for example one decides what is missing from the kitchen shelves and later recalls the missing items at the shops. However, it is also used of situations in which there is no particular event to which one has paid attention; for example, one tries to remember the correct word to use in a particular context. Moreover, there are also occasions when one has paid attention to something to the extent that one would be capable, if asked, of recalling it; for example one might watch a film without the intention of giving an account of it subsequently, but nevertheless be potentially capable of doing so if asked.

In the field of experimental psychology, the area described as memory research employs the technique of presenting material to subjects and subsequently demanding its recognition or recall. It thus resembles the first of the situations described above. However, this does not imply that the psychological processes revealed by the use of this technique are not concerned in other experimental situations. The processes evidenced in memory experiments may be involved in experiments concerning attention, perception, and retrieval.

The term process has already been employed several times, and requires definition. It refers to a series of events which form an entity. The connexion between the events is primarily temporal – they occur in a sequence in time. The criterion for stating that one process is distinct from another process is whether independent variables have qualitatively different effects. For example, one process may be affected by phonological but not semantic features of material, while the reverse may be true of another. One obvious result of this rationale is that as experimental techniques become more sophisticated, what was previously thought to be a process will be seen to consist of several different processes. The processes with which this book is concerned are assumed to be cortical functions; but whether they have specifiable physiological correlates remains to be seen.

It should be stressed that a complete and detailed model of memory processes is not available or maybe even possible. Several different detailed models are at present under discussion (1). Arguments about the relative merits of different models are interesting, but irrelevant to the basic concerns of this book. What will now be presented is an overall summary in a very abbreviated form of the areas of basic agreement. Only review articles or books will be cited in this chapter.

It is generally agreed that *coding* processes are implicated in all memory tasks (2, 10). Coding means that subjects transform the material from its presented form to some other form. Thus it is important not to confound the nominal stimulus, the material as presented, with the functional stimulus, the material as coded. Coding may take many different forms. It may, for example, involve the use by the subject of the auditory or visual characteristics of the material presented (3). He may code an item in terms of its position in relation to other items that were also presented, or in terms of other words which are closely associated with it in his vocabulary. Or he may employ the item's position along several dimensions of connotative meaning. For example, he may code the auditorily presented item navy in terms of its initial sound, its position subsequent in the presented list to the item house, its association with the word sailor, and a negative evaluative response.

It is still a matter for debate how many different aspects, attributes, of features of the material are employed in coding. Their number and nature may well depend upon the nature of the memory task (4). However, two functions of coding have been specified. Coding may be *reductive*. That is, a single coding may contain the equivalent amount of information to several presented items. Coding therefore reduces the load on the limited capacity information channel of the human subject (5). On the other hand, coding may also be *elaborative*. That is, many attributes of an item may be used to code it in order to ensure that, when recall is required, the correct item can be retrieved from the many closely related items which are also part of the subject's repertoire. The attributes thus uniquely specify the item, so retrieval of the correct item is possible.

When several items are presented, it is probable that some of them have attributes in common by which they may be coded as a group. This coding of several items together by a common attribute will be termed *secondary process* in this book. The term organisation refers to the relations between the items which the subject perceives in the material (9).

The function of secondary process may well be primarily reductive. Clearly, the coding of a relation between items will require less processing capacity than separate codings for each of the items. On the other hand, the items themselves must be coded individually to some extent in order for the correct items to be retrieved and recalled. To take an example, if a list of thirty words to be recalled contains five animals, then the semantic relation between those items (that they are animals) may be used to code them. On the other hand, one has to recall the correct five animals, and not any others of the large class of animals. Nevertheless, it seems evident that secondary processes should aid memory (see Chapter 3). For they reduce the load on the system, and provide codings which should help in retrieving items for recall; a general coding, such as animals, reduces the number of alternatives from which the correct item to be recalled has to be selected.

The major difficulties concern the distinction between the experimenter's expectations of the nature of the subject's organisation, and the subject's actual organisation in practise (7). The experimenter may select material which can be organised in a certain way, and he may measure subjects' recall to see if they have organised it in that way. But it is quite possible that the subject has employed many other attributes of the material and organised it in quite different and highly complex ways. To take a very obvious example, the experimenter uses measures of organisation which imply that a given item is organised as part of a single group of items only; but it is quite possible that an item may be coded in terms of several different groups of items. Another difficulty concerns the extent to which secondary process is unconsciously applied and the extent to which it is the result of consciously selected strategies. Experimenters who have been interested in specifying the structural characteristics of the human information – processing system have concentrated on the former, treating conscious strategies as confounding variables. But it may be the case that so much memory performance is the result of conscious strategies that it is impossible to leave them out of account.

b. Memory research

Knowledge about secondary process has been advanced in particular by the use of the technique of free recall (6,7). Subjects are free to recall items in any order they wish. This permits the amount recalled to be distinguished from the order in which items are recalled. An analysis of the order of items permits organisation to be described. That this organisation has been imposed by the subject is clear from the fact that while presentation of items is in random order, their recall is principled.

The amount of organisation imposed by the subject can be measured. Furthermore, measures are available which permit organisation to be assessed independently of amount recalled. Any positive correlation between degree of organisation and amount recalled will then avoid being a statistical artefact. However, it must be stressed that measures do not always faithfully reflect organisation. Therefore it is important to distinguish organisation (the structure placed by the subject on the material) from measures.

The measures habitually employed will be termed clustering, when they are indices of the extent to which items are recalled in experimenter-defined groupings on any recall trial (see Appendix 1); and inter-trial repetition (ITR), which is an attempted measure of the extent to which apparently unrelated items are recalled in the same order on successive trials (see Appendix 1). Measures of organisation thus attempt to index organisation imposed by the experimenter on the material and on the analysis of the order of recall; and organisation imposed by the subject on material selected by the experimenter for its apparent lack of relations.

Given that the major dependent variables are amount recalled and order of recall, the function of the independent variables is to produce such different effects upon them as to enable the experimenter to distinguish different processes. One major independent variable is time; the period between presentation and recall is manipulated by the experimenter with markedly different results on such variables as number of items recalled. However, it should be stressed that the presentation-recall interval itself is not grounds for postulating different processes; one cannot hypothesise different memory processes merely because one can require immediate or delayed recall. Other typical independent variables are the amount and type of material presented; the sensory modality in which it is presented; the rate at which it is presented; whether presentation of items is item by item or simultaneous; whether the experimenter presents items in a random or a principled order; whether he selects the material with some sort of organisation already inherent in it, or whether items are randomly selected; whether he provides other cues which may assist the subject; or whether, on the contrary, he presents other material in addition to the material to be recalled which interferes with recall.

The choice of which independent variables to manipulate obviously depends upon the nature of the inferences to be made. Thus, for example, if one wishes to infer that many different types of organisation inherent in the material may be employed by the subject, one will manipulate the type of material presented.

The term cue is used here of a certain specific type of experimenter intervention, that is, the provision of items other than the items to be recalled. These additional items are designed to facilitate recall, not to interfere with it. They may have connexions with individual items only or they may be tags for relations between items. They should be distinguished, firstly, from other forms of experimenter intervention such as presentation of items in a principled way. Secondly, they should be distinguished from codings, which are essentially subject-imposed rather than experimenter-provided. Thus cues may be codings, in the sense that the subject may use for himself the cues provided; but codings need not be cues, for the subject could use other codings than the cues provided.

Cues have usually been used in an effort to distinguish processes of storage, retention, and retrieval (see p. 13). The interpretation of results derived from their use requires caution, however (see p. 14). Moreover, certain manipulations of the presentation and recall phases of the experiment have been employed to the same end. The usual experimental procedure is to use several cycles of the presentation-recall sequence, i.e. presentation, recall, presentation, recall, presentation, recall (etc.) This is termed multi-trial free recall. However, if the experimenter wishes, for example, to stress the presentation phase (and, by implication, the storage process), he may give several presentation trials followed by a recall trial. It should be stressed, however, that presentation is not synonymous with storage, nor recall with retrieval (see p. 15). Presentation and recall are features of a memory task, but storage and retrieval are inferred aspects of processes.

It should also be stressed that experimental memory research has its shortcomings. Material consists of items rather than meaningful wholes, despite Bartlett's strictures (8). Subjects are usually college students. Recall is demanded as an end rather than as a means to an end. Motivation for an experimental task as an end may be different from motivation for a task to which memory is a means. In brief, the balance between scientific control and generalisability of results has perhaps tilted towards control.

References

1. NORMAN, D.A. (1969) (Ed.). *Models of Memory.* New York, Academic Press.
2. NEISSER, U. (1967). *Cognitive Psychology.* New York, Appleton-Century-Crofts.
3. CRAIK, F.I.M. (1971). 'Primary memory.' *British Medical Bulletin,* 27, 232-236.
4. CRAIK, F.I.M. and LOCKHART, R.S. (1972). 'Levels of processing: A framework for memory research'. *Journal of Verbal Learning and Verbal Behavior,* 11, 671-684.
5. ATKINSON, R.C. and SHIFFRIN, R.M. (1968). 'A proposed system and its control processes.' In SPENCE, K.W. and SPENCE, J.T. (Eds.) *The Psychology of Learning and Motivation: Advances in Research and Theory.* Vol. 2. New York, Academic Press.
6. SHUELL, T.J. (1969). 'Clustering and organisation in free recall.' Psychological Bulletin, 72, 353-374.
7. TULVING, E. (1968). 'Theoretical issues in free recall.' In DIXON, T.H. and HORTON, D.L. (Eds.) *Verbal Behavior and General Behavior Theory.* Englewood Cliffs, N.J. Prentice-Hall.
8. BARTLETT, F. (1932). *Remembering.* Cambridge, Cambridge University Press.
9. TULVING, E. and DONALDSON, W. (1972) (Eds.). *Organisation of Memory.* New York, Academic Press.
10. MELTON, A.W. and MARTIN, E. (1972) (Eds.). *Coding Processes in Human Memory.* Washington, D.C. Winston.

Chapter 2

Organisation

a. When is it used?

Considerable evidence is now available that subjects organise material when they are given the free recall task described in the previous chapter. The first two sections of this chapter will be concerned with evidence derived from experiments in which different types of material are presented in random order and recalled in principled order. This is the strongest sort of evidence for organisation which is available. Unfortunately, it does not usually enable the experimenter to distinguish sub-processes within secondary processes. The third section will deal with the various types of intervention by the experimenter which have been employed in an effort to evidence sub-processes; in particular, it will discuss efforts to distinguish storage and retrieval.

In general, if there is any basis for organising the material, this will be used in the recall of the items. However, this assumes that the number of items and the length of time between presentation and recall render it necessary to employ secondary processes, other coding processes being inadequate on their own. Granted this assumption, the first experimental evidence using the free recall technique employed categorical material (1). Subsequently the following materials have been presented: words with associative relations with other words (2); words of different frequency of occurrence (3); words of different taxonomic frequency (i.e. words cited as instances of a category commonly or more rarely) (4); pairs of words of different logical relationship to each other (e.g. subordinate, co-ordinate, superordinate) (5); words of different grammatical form class (6); synonyms (7); words commencing each with a different letter of the alphabet (8); words represented by pictures of similar shape (9); and words with a similar imagery component (10); the organisation implicit in all these materials has been used by subjects in recall, to a greater or lesser degree. It should be stressed, however, that this does not imply a different process for each type of material; one does not have to hypothesise a categorical or an associationist process (11). Rather, the fact that such different types of material can be organised implies that the processes postulated to account for the organisation must hold for many different tasks.

One interesting area of research concerns the organisation by subjects of material which the experimenter has selected on a random basis. There is consistency over trials in the order in which they recall items, despite random-order presentation (12). Subjects, in other words, impose structure on material deliberately chosen so as to be unstructured. The most striking findings employ the interference paradigm; that is, the effects of the learning of one set of material upon the learning of another set of material is observed. When a part of a list is learned, followed by the learning of the whole list, proactive interference of the part on the whole is found (13,14); subjects who had learned the part list subsequently recalled less of the whole list after several trials than subjects who had not. The inference is that the organisation applied to the part list is inappropriate when the items are interspersed with others, as in the whole list. If recall were a matter of familiarisation with individual items as items, facilitation rather than interference would be predicted. It can be inferred from these results that the organisation which subjects use covers the whole list; for even when the part list consists of three-quarters of the whole list, interference still occurs (15). Interference from whole to part list also occurs (16). The only situation in which interference does not occur is when the whole list is presented in such a way that the part list organisation is still appropriate (17,18). It should be stressed that in these experiments using an interference paradigm, organisation has to be inferred from amount recalled rather than observed and measured in recall.

Thus, not only is the organisation imposed by subjects on a list of 'unrelated' items widespread; it is also persistent. It becomes more and more difficult to impose another organisation upon a subject who has started to learn using his own organisation (19); and subjects take far longer to sort and learn items according to other subjects' sorting than according to their own (20). Nevertheless, the organisation is not totally peculiar to each individual, since there is some degree of commonality in the order in which subjects recall items at the end of a multi-trial series (21,22).

Thus far, it has been shown that the organisation imposed by secondary processes can be of many different types. In the case of experimenter-defined structure, subjects can perceive and utilise many types of relation. In the case of apparently unrelated items, subjects impose their own organisation; this organisation may have its origins in shared associative networks. It has also been shown that organisation is widespread over the list of items presented, and that it is difficult to reverse once the subject has applied it.

b. *Features of organisation*

What more concrete generalisations can be made about subjects' use of organisation? The first important point is that subjects have available a variety of *strategies* when the task demands their use. That is, when secondary processes have to be employed, subjects can draw upon several techniques to assist them. For example, they can employ a serial strategy, remembering a list by employing each item to cue the next; or they can employ mediators, that is, words commonly associated with more than one of the items, to link those items together; or they can analyse the material in terms of categories and items. Indeed, they might employ more than one of these strategies simultaneously.

There is evidence to show that the use of a strategy improves with practise; and that subjects are conscious of the fact that they are using strategies.

Firstly, evidence of improvement with practise. When both items and categories are different on subsequent sessions, increased organisation occurs over sessions. This is true of categorically related items (23,24,25) and of unrelated items (26). Moreover, organisation of a particular set of items may increase as a result of prior recall trials as well as of prior presentation trials (27,28,29), implying that practise in applying organisation increases the use subjects make of it. Care must be taken, however, not to confound the effects of recall trials with those of time (30). The fact that subjects may be consciously using organisation is clear from experiments which use introspective reports by subjects as the dependent variable (31,32,33).

However, it should be stressed that organisation is seldom optimal; subjects seldom recall precisely in the order imposed on the material by the experimenter. This is probably because the organisation provided by the experimenter is not obvious at presentation. Thus, for example, simultaneous presentation of items results in more organisation than sequential (34), since relations may be more evident when items are available together. Visually presented items are organised more than auditorily presented ones (35), perhaps because visual presentation permits more common features between items to be perceived. Another reason for non-optimal organisation could be that subjects are not familiar with the relations provided in the material by the experimenter, or else wish to use their own idiosyncratic organisation. These possibilities must be particularly emphasised when subjects are children (chapter 4) or subnormals (chapter 5). A final possible reason is that too many items or too short a period of presentation prevent all the relations being perceived.

Coding has already been mentioned as an essential feature of memory processes (see p. 4). If the coding is of relations between items rather than of items themselves, then its function of reducing information load is apparent. The connexions between organisation and amount recalled will be discussed in chapter 3. Here we are concerned with evidence that coding of relations does occur. Most of the evidence refers to categorisable material, since it is assumed that subjects have the category coding potentially available; but there is no reason in principle why it should not refer to other types of material as well.

One very strong piece of evidence for codings of relations is that when interfering material is presented, interference is at a category, rather than at an item level (36). That is, fewer categories are recalled rather than fewer items per category (37); moreover, the effects of interference may be counteracted by the provision of cues (38). Other interesting evidence for coding of relations is derived from experiments which observe the temporal characteristics of recall. It has been found that items within a category cluster are recalled in short bursts, with little time between items, but a greater interval between the last item of one category and the first of the next (39,40). Moreover, the time interval between categories increases as the recall trial progresses (41). In both cases, coding of relations is implicated, as it is in a related experiment; when category labels were presented as items to be recalled together with the items they subsume, they were recalled at the head of a cluster of items (42).

A final piece of evidence for coding is the 'some or none' effect (43). That is, either several items from a given category are recalled or none at all. This implies that a coding of relations (possibly a category label) is employed by the subject to organise items. Indeed, such a coding may result in as many different categories being recalled when the material is categorisable as items when it is not (44). This finding implies that when organisation is easily perceived and codings are immediately available, it is the codings rather than the items which are retained.

However, it is less clear what the *relations* are between codings of relations and items (strictly, codings of items). Evidence suggests that while codings are used hierarchically to chunk related items together, items may be related sequentially as well. That is, an item may cue another item. At any rate, sequential processes as indexed by the ITR measure are present when categorical material is recalled (45,46). That is, there is some consistency from trial to trial in the order in which items are recalled. Evidence that both sequential and hierarchical relations are involved is available in the recall of linguistically structured material (47).

More important, there are connexions between codings of relations themselves. These connexions may be sequential in nature (48); in other words each coding may cue the next. Such a strategy would be particularly expected when the codings were of categories or other groupings which were not apparently related to each other. However, they may also be hierarchical; in other words, there may be codings of codings. Such an organisation would be appropriate where the subject could impose superordinate codings because of the tree structure of the material; for example, where the items were all minerals, but there were sub-categories and sub-categories of those (49,50). Subjects employ the lower-level categories to start with, but on later trials start to use higher-level ones (51). Perhaps, instead of speaking of codings as though they were independent, it would be preferable to speak of a single organisation covering the whole list (52). This is true both of categorisable and apparently unrelated lists (see p. 10).

Specific features of organisation which have emerged in the present section are, firstly, that when the need to use organisation arises, subjects have strategies available; they can improve their efficiency at using strategies, and they can be conscious that they are using them. Codings of relations are implied by the use of organisation, and these codings are connected to each other.

c. *Storage, retention and retrieval*

Evidence has become available (see chapter 3) which shows that a considerable number of items are potentially available for recall, but are not actually recalled unless the experimenter provides cues at recall. This has led to a stress on the retrieval of items at recall, and to efforts to distinguish storage and retrieval sub-processes.

One popular approach (53) is to suggest that perception and coding of relations occur at presentation; the codings, or codings of codings, are retained; and when recall is required, the codings are used to retrieve items (or, strictly speaking, codings of items). The items which have been retrieved are subjected to a recognition check, in order to ensure that they were actually among the items presented. An alternative hypothesis (54) maintains that items are stored individually, and that when recall is required, a retrieval plan is devised.

These are hypotheses to account for what usually occurs. However, it would be true to say that most experiments have provided evidence of what can occur rather than what usually occurs. This is because they employ cues (see p. 7), or other forms of experimenter intervention. It is therefore worth considering the inferences which can legitimately be made from this sort of experimental manipulation. If subjects organise or recall more when they are provided with a cue than when they are not, what does this imply?

One inference that has been made is that cues demonstrate processes which are habitually employed. Thus, suppose cues are provided at the presentation phase only, or at both presentation and recall phases (55). If the latter condition results in greater recall than the former, this could be attributed to the fact that the experimenter is doing what the subject usually does for himself, but is doing it better. Thus the specific inference here would be that the retention of codings and their use for retrieval are particularly important since cues at recall lead to such improvement. However, if subjects do habitually apply codings at presentation, retain them, and use them for retrieval, why should their provision at recall lead to such an improvement? Clearly, to say the least, their retention of codings must be far from optimal if facilitation is so clearly evidenced.

The contrary inference is equally popular (see pp. 45-6). It is that cues facilitate organisation or amount recalled because the subject is in some way deficient in the process which the cue is aimed to assist. Thus, for example, if material is presented in such a way that the relations between items are made more apparent, it is tempting to infer that subjects whose recall is facilitated are deficient in perceiving and utilising the relations between items (56). This type of inference assumes that the cues in some sense perform the process for the subject rather than elicit it; and therefore, since he can only succeed when it is done for him, he cannot do it himself.

A preferable type of inference is that the facilitatory effect of cues indicates that an available process is capable of being used more effectively Thus in the case of the experiment employing cues at recall as well as at presentation, the inference would be as follows; when recall cues are provided, retrieval of items by means of those cues is enhanced. Therefore retrieval is potentially a highly efficient process. Or in the case of the experiment providing structure at presentation, the inferences are that, given cues, subjects can perceive relations; and that having perceived them, they can utilise them for storage and retrieval. It must be admitted that some forms of experimenter intervention do perform the operation for the subject. For example, in cases where the experimenter instructs the subject to use categorical relations to assist his recall, he has selected the subject's strategy for him. Thus there is no inference possible that the subject can select a suitable strategy given help. However, the inference is possible that, once the strategy has been selected for him, he can use it effectively.

Thus considerable caution has to be exercised in interpreting the results of experiments employing cues. A facilitatory result *may* indicate that the process directly affected by the cue is potentially more efficient. It will also indicate that certain other processes are functioning adequately. This is because the only evidence of process is at recall; therefore all those processes which intervene between the process directly affected by the cue and recall are also implicated. To quote the experiment previously cited by way of example: the additional structure provided by the experimenter showed that subjects could, given help, perceive relations at presentation; but it also shows that their retention and retrieval were adequate to cope with this additional information, since perception of the relations was evidenced in recall. This dicussion is carried further on page 46.

Cues have been employed in efforts to distinguish storage, retention, and retrieval processes. In addition to the hazards of interpretation described above, additional difficulties occur with the free recall procedure. Consider, for example, the case of category cues provided at presentation. Since the only evidence of their effect is the order of items in recall, it cannot be inferred that these presentation cues were employed to assist organisation at storage. Rather, items and cues may have been stored independently, and then the cues used as a retrieval plan by which items were organised at recall. Consider, secondly, cues provided at recall. It cannot be inferred from the fact that they result in increased organisation that the organisation has been applied at recall; for subjects might have applied the organisation at presentation without assistance, the recall cues thus serving only to reinstate it. In brief, presentation is not synonymous with storage, nor recall with retrieval; the former are features of a memory task, the latter are inferred aspects of processes.

Thus the vast majority of experiments employing cues must be construed as follows; the many types of cue provided and the several points within the free recall task at which they are effective demonstrate the variability of the processes available and their potentially immense efficiency. Most cues and other forms of assistance have been provided at presentation. Presentation has been in hierarchically organised format (50,51,57); or with items from the same experimenter-defined grouping presented together in time or space (58,59,60). The importance of these experiments is not that they indicate the relative importance of storage and retrieval. It is rather that they show that the benefit of the cues provided at presentation obtains throughout the task; the potential to use such organisation for recall is there.

However, it is possible that the subject can select a strategy at recall, even when a different strategy has been selected for him at presentation. Thus, when serial recall instructions were given at presentation, but free recall instructions at recall, organisation was evidenced at recall; it was also evidenced when recall cues were given (61).

In summary, the organisation implicit in all sorts of material, including material particularly selected as having no apparent organisation at all, can be used in memory. The structure which subjects impose on material is widespread and persistent. Subjects employ different strategies to make use of organisation; these may be consciously employed and improve with practice. Organisation involves coding of relations by subjects, which may also be related to each other by codings of codings. There are difficulties in distinguishing the sub-processes of storage, retention and retrieval; for inferences which may be drawn from the experimenter's use of cues or other interventions are ambiguous.

References

1. BOUSFIELD, W.A. (1953). 'The occurrence of clustering in the recall of randomly arranged associates.' *Journal of General Psychology*, **49**, 229-240.
2. MARSHALL, G.R. (1967). 'Stimulus characteristics contributing to organisation in free recall.' *Journal of Verbal Learning and Verbal Behavior*, 6, 364-374.
3. BOUSFIELD, W.A. and COHEN, B.H. (1955). 'The occurrence of clustering in the recall of randomly arranged words of different frequencies of usage.' *Journal of General Psychology*, **52**, 83-95.

4. BOUSFIELD, W.A., COHEN, B.H., and WHITMARSH, G.A. (1958). 'Associative clustering in the recall of words of different taxonomic frequencies of occurrence.' Psychological Reports, **4**, 39-44.
5. QUAINTANCE, B. and SHAPIRO, S.I. (1970). 'The influence of class membership, method of presentation, and restricted association strength, on free recall learning.' Canadian Journal of Psychology, **24**, 70-76.
6. STANNERS, R.F. (1969). 'Grammatical organisation in free recall.' Journal of Verbal Learning and Verbal Behavior, 8, 95-100.
7. COFER, C.N. (1959). 'A study of clustering in free recall based on synonyms.' *Journal of General Psychology*, **60**, 3-10.
8. TULVING, E. (1962). 'The effect of alphabetical subjective organisation on memorising unrelated words.' *Canadian Journal of Psychology*, **16**, 185-191.
9. FROST, N. (1971). 'Clustering by visual shape in the free recall of pictorial stimuli.' *Journal of Experimental Psychology*, **88**, 409-413.
10. WALKER, H.R. (1971). 'Interaction of imagery, associative overlap, and category membership in multi-trial free recall.' *Journal of Experimental Psychology*, **88**, 333-339.
11. POSTMAN, L. (1964). 'Short-term memory and incidental learning.' In A.W. MELTON (Ed.) *Categories of Human Learning*. New York, Academic Press.
12. TULVING, E. (1962), 'Subjective organisation in free recall of "unrelated" words.'*Psychological Review*, **69**, 344-354.
13. TULVING, E. (1966). 'Subjective organisation and effects of repetition in multi-trial free-recall learning.' *Journal of Verbal Learning and Verbal Behavior*, **5**, 193-197.
14. BIRNBAUM, I.M. (1968). 'Free-recall learning as a function of prior-list organisation.' *Journal of Verbal Learning and Verbal Behavior*, 7, 1037-1042.
15. EHRLICH, S. (1970). 'Structuration and destructuration of responses in free recall learning.' *Journal of Verbal Learning and Verbal Behavior*, **9**, 282-286.
16. NOVINSKI, L. (1969). 'Part-whole and whole-part free recall learning.' *Journal of Verbal Learning and Verbal Behavior*, **8**, 152-154.
17. BOWER, G.H. and LESGOLD, A.M. (1969). 'Organisation as

a determinant of part-to-whole transfer in free recall.' *Journal of Verbal Learning and Verbal Behavior,* 8, 501-506.

18. ORNSTEIN, P.A. (1970). 'Role of prior-list organisation in a free-recall transfer task.' *Journal of Experimental Psychology,* **86**, 32-37.
19. EARHARD, M. (1969). 'Storage and retrieval of words encoded in memory.' *Journal of Experimental Psychology,* **80**, 412-418.
20. MANDLER, G., and PEARLSTONE, Z. (1966). 'Free and constrained concept learning and subsequent recall.' *Journal of Verbal Learning and Verbal Behavior,* **5**, 126-131.
21. BOUSFIELD, W.A., PUFF, C.R. and COWAN, T.M. (1964). 'The development of constancies in sequential organisation during repeated free recall.' *Journal of Verbal Learning and Verbal Behavior,* **3**, 489-495.
22. BOUSFIELD, W.A. and ABRAMCYZK, R.R. (1966). 'Sequential ordering in repeated free recall as a function of the length of the stimulus word list.' *Canadian Journal of Psychology,* **20**, 427-434.
23. THOMPSON, C.P. and ROENKER, D.L. (1971).'Learning to cluster.' *Journal of Experimental Psychology,* **91**, 136-139.
24. ROBERTS, W.A. and SMITH, I. (1966). 'The effects of categorization and categorical repetition on successive recalls of word lists.' *Psychonomic Science,* **5**, 225-226.
25. GEROW, J.R. (1970). 'Learning the rules of categorized free recall.' *Psychonomic Science,* **20**, 79-80.
26. MAYHEW, A.J. (1967). 'Interlist changes in subjective organisation during free recall learning.' *Journal of Experimental Psychology,* **74**, 425-430.
27. TULVING, E. (1967). 'The effects of presentation and recall of material in free recall learning.' *Journal of Verbal Learning and Verbal Behavior,* **6**, 175-184.
28. LACHMAN, R. and LAUGHERY, K.R. (1968). 'Is a test trial a training trial in free recall learning?' *Journal of Experimental Psychology,* **76**, 40-50.
29. ROSNER, S.R. (1970). 'The effects of presentation and recall trials on organisation in multi-trial free recall.' *Journal of Verbal Learning and Verbal Behavior,* **9**, 69-74.
30. COKE, E.U. (1971). 'The effects of test events and spaced practice on free recall learning.' *Psychonomic Science,* **22**, 335-336.

31. EAGLE, M.N. (1967). 'The effect of learning strategies upon free recall.' *American Journal of Psychology*, **80**, 421-425.
32. LOEB, J.W. and DENIKE, L.D. (1969). 'Prediction of organisation in free recall from reported learning strategy.' *Psychological Reports*, **25**, 631-636.
33. STOFF, D.M. and EAGLE, M.N. (1971). 'The relationship among reported strategies, presentation rate, and verbal ability, and their effects on free recall learning.' *Journal of Experimental Psychology*, 87, 423-428.
34. PUFF, C.R. and BOUSFIELD, W.A. (1967). 'Development of intertrial organisation with simultaneous presentation of stimulus items.' *Journal of Verbal Learning and Verbal Behavior*, **6**, 213-215.
35. SCOTT, K.G. (1967). 'Clustering with perceptual and symbolic stimuli in free recall.' *Journal of Verbal Learning and Verbal Behavior*, **6**, 864-866.
36. STRAND, B.Z. (1971). 'Further investigation of retroactive inhibition in categorized free recall.' *Journal of Experimental Psychology*, **87**, 198-201.
37. WINOGRAD, E. (1968). 'List differentiation, recall and category similarity.' *Journal of Experimental Psychology*, **78**, 510-515.
38 TULVING; E. and PSOTKA, J. (1971). 'Retroactive inhibition in free recall: inaccessibility of information available in the memory store.' *Journal of Experimental Psychology*, **87**, 1-8.
39 POLLIO, H.R., RICHARDS, S. and LUCAS, R. (1969). 'Temporal properties of category recall.' *Journal of Verbal Learning and Verbal Behavior*, **8**, 529-536.
40. POLLIO, H.R. and FOOTE, R. (1971). 'Memory as a reconstructive process.' *British Journal of Psychology*, **62**, 53-58.
41. PATTERSON, K.E., MELTZER, R.H. and MANDLER, G. (1971). 'Inter-response times in categorized free recall.' *Journal of Verbal Learning and Verbal Behavior*, **10**, 417-426.
42. SEGAL, E.M. (1969). 'Hierarchical structure in free recall.' *Journal of Experimental Psychology*, **80**, 59-63.
43. COHEN, B.H. (1966). 'Some or none characteristics of coding.' *Journal of Verbal Learning and Verbal Behavior*, **5**, 182-187.
44. COHEN, B.H. (1963). 'Recall of categorized word lists.' *Journal of Experimental Psychology*, **66**, 227-234.

45. MANDLER, G. (1969). 'Input variables and output strategies in free recall of categorised lists.' *American Journal of Psychology*, **82**, 531-539.
46. PUFF, C.R. (1970). 'An investigation of two forms of organisation in free recall.' *Journal of Verbal Learning and Verbal Behavior*, **9**, 720-724.
47. JOHNSON, N.R. (1966). 'Linguistic models and functional units of language behavior.' In S. ROSENBERG (Ed.) *Directions in Psycholinguistics*, New York, Macmillan.
48. ROBINSON, J.A. (1966). 'Category clustering on free recall.' *Journal of Psychology*, **62**, 279-285.
49. BOWER, G.H., CLARK, M.C., LESGOLD, A.M. and WINZENZ, D. (1969). 'Hierarchical retrieval schemes in recall of categorized word lists.' *Journal of Verbal Learning and Verbal Behavior*, **8**, 323-343.
50. COHEN, B.H. and BOUSFIELD, W.A. (1956). 'The effects of a dual-level stimulus word list on the occurrence of clustering in free recall.' *Journal of General Psychology*, **55**, 51-58.
51. WORTMAN, P.M. and GREENBERG, L.D. (1971). 'Coding, recoding, and decoding of hierarchical information in long-term memory.' *Journal of Verbal Learning and Verbal Behavior*, **10**, 234-243.
52. WOOD, G. (1971). 'Organisation, large memory units, and free recall.' *Journal of Verbal Learning and Verbal Behavior*, **10**, 52-56.
53. TULVING, E. (1968). 'Theoretical issues in free recall.' In T.H. DIXON and D.L. HORTON, (Eds.) *Verbal Behavior and General Behavior Theory*. Englewood Cliffs, N.J., Prentice-Hall.
54. SLAMECKA, J. (1968). 'An examination of trace storage in free recall.' *Journal of Experimental Psychology*, **76**, 504-513.
55. TULVING, E. and PEARLSTONE, Z. (1966). 'Availability versus accessibility of information in memory for words.' *Journal of Verbal Learning and Verbal Behavior*, **5**, 381-391.
56. GERJOUY, I.R. and SPITZ, H.H. (1966). 'Associative clustering in free recall: intellectual and developmental variables.' *American Journal of Mental Deficiency*, **70**, 918-927.
57. PREUSSER, D. and HANDEL, S. (1970). 'The free classification of hierarchically and categorically related stimuli.' *Journal of Verbal Learning and Verbal Behavior*, **9**, 222-231.
58. PUFF, C.R. (1966). 'Clustering as a function of the sequential

organisation of stimulus word lists.' *Journal of Verbal Learning and Verbal Behavior,* **5**, 503-506.

59. COFER, C.N., BRUCE, D.R. and REICHER, G.M. (1966). 'Clustering in free recall as a function of certain methodological variables.' *Journal of Experimental Psychology,* **71**, 858-866.

60. DREW, C.J. and ALTMAN, R. (1970). 'Effects of input organisation and material difficulty on free recall.' *Psychological Reports,* **27**, 335-337.

61. BRUDER, G., LATTANZIO, S. and MELTZER, J. (1971). 'Differences in free and serial recall of categorized lists.' *Journal of Verbal Learning and Verbal Behavior,* **10**, 386-391.

Chapter 3

Organisation and amount recalled

a. *Evidence for a positive relationship*

The view of organisation presented in the previous chapter suggests immediately that when information processing capacity is stretched, increased use of organisation should result in an increase in amount recalled. If organisation involves the coding of relations between items, such codings will reduce the amount of information with which the subject has to deal, for he need only deal with relations, rather than items. Furthermore, they will result in the retrieval of more items for recall, since items do not each have to be retrieved individually by means of their own coding; rather, the same coding can retrieve several items.

However, the process of coding must be efficient if such benefits are to be obtained in retention and retrieval. Consider first, for example, the case in which the subject simply applies category labels to category members. If there are twelve categories within the list, he will have to retain twelve individual category labels. Clearly, coding of codings would be required if information load is to be reduced sufficiently. In other words, the category labels themselves would have to be retrieved by means of a yet higher-order coding. Consider, secondly, the case in which the category labels are not sufficiently familiar as superordinates of their items. In this case, even if the subject retains them adequately, he may not be able to retrieve items by their use, since the relation between coding and items is not adequately established. Sufficient information reduction (and thus improved recall) can only be ensured if coding is adequate.

It is the thesis of this chapter that in principle organisation should increase amount recalled. The relation is not consistently found in practise because the degree of efficiency of coding has more effect on amount recalled than on degree of organisation; further, organisation is indexed by ordering of recall, and ordering may involve certain additional skills. However, it is maintained that inefficient coding at presentation is more likely to be a function of extrinsic task variables than an intrinsic failure of the system. It is concluded, in other words, that though capacity for information may be limited, strategies for reducing information load to manageable proportions by organising the material are potentially available. For, as has been shown in Chapter 2, many complex ways of coding codings can be devised by subjects.

The evidence supporting the existence of a relationship between degree of organisation and amount recalled will now be reviewed. Perhaps the most convincing are the findings that nearly all the independent variables which result in effects on organisation also result in effects on amount recalled. Blocked presentation of categorically related items, information that organisation is applicable, cues at presentation, cues at presentation and recall, inter-item associative strength, mediated associations, meaningfulness, and taxonomic frequency all increase amount recalled (for references, see p. 9).

Secondly, a positive correlation between degree of organisation and amount recalled has been repeatedly found for all the subjects employed within any one experiment. This is particularly true of material which can be categorically organised. However, this is conditional upon a limitation on the number of categories (1, 2, 3) and the number of items per category (3,4). Correlations between the ITR measure of organisation of 'unrelated' items and amount recalled have also been found (5,6).

Thirdly, an important source of positive evidence is the series of experiments using cues at recall which was initiated by Tulving and Pearlstone's key work (7). They found that category labels provided as cues by the experimenter both at presentation and at recall led to greater recall than cues provided at presentation only. Furthermore, this difference in amount recalled resulted from an increase in the number of categories recalled, not from an increase in the number of items per category. In other words, the provision of cues assisted the subjects' retention of codings rather than their retrieval of items by means of the codings. The reason for this improvement thus seems clear: subjects had difficulty in retaining the cues they had been provided with at presentation, so when the experimenter, as it were, retained the cues for the subject, more categories were recalled. However, it has been shown that subjects can code codings so that what they have to retain is reduced to manageable proportions. Therefore it seems reasonable to suppose that there were aspects of the Tulving and Pearlstone experiment which made it difficult for such codings to occur. For example the categories were unrelated to each other, so a higher level organisation would be more difficult to impose. Duration of presentation may have been too limited to permit higher order coding to take place.

This interpretation of the Tulving and Pearlstone experiment is at first sight confounded by experiments which show that recall cues alone can increase amount recalled (8, 9). However, this result only obtains when the items have a high taxonomic frequency of occurrence or are of high associative relatedness. In these cases it seems reasonable to assume that subjects provided their own codings at presentation which were the same as, or sufficiently similar to, the cues the experimenter provided at recall (10). When the organisation in the material is less obvious, cues provided at recall can interfere with the subject's own organisation imposed at presentation (11, 12, 13). Thus it still seems possible to maintain that recall cues improve amount recalled because they retain the subject's codings imposed at presentation and reinstate them for him when he needs to recall. The inference is that the degree of organisation imposed by the subject at presentation is inadequate, since it does not permit him to retain his codings; information load, in other words, needs to be reduced still further. Therefore the experiments showing a facilitatory effect of recall cues are evidence that there are circumstances which prevent subjects from exercising their full organisational skill. Assistance from the experimenter results in the increase in recall which would have resulted from the subjects' own organisational efforts.

The experiments just described show how number of categories recalled can be increased. Work which will now be considered reveals that number of items per category can also be increased. Prior recall trials result in more items per category being recalled in subsequent recall trials (14). In other words, repeated opportunities to use codings for retrieval result in greater accessibility of items for retrieval. The inference is that access to items is not an all or none matter; it may vary with the degree of association between cue or coding and item; and with the number of possible alternative items from which the coding has to retrieve the items to be recalled.

At presentation the subject needs to establish close connections between a coding and its items such that the coding can retrieve those items. Usually these close connections are already potentially available in the subject's verbal repertoire. He does not need to learn the coding-item associations, but rather to *select* a coding which already has strong associations with the items.

If the coding fails by retrieving items other than those presented, a recognition check may be applied which prevents their overt recall. There is some possibility that this check works on a simple discriminative basis. That is, after a coding has retrieved an item, it is checked to see if it is recognised as one of the items presented or not (15, 16). Alternatively, it is possible that a double check is operated – not only 'Was this item presented or not?' but also 'Does the coding generate this item or not?' (17) Clearly, a recognition check will be more necessary if the codings are related to many items in addition to the ones presented.

At any rate, the use of different sorts of cue at recall to facilitate amount recalled has demonstrated that coding by the subject at presentation must be efficient. It has indicated two particular ways in which skill in coding is required. Firstly, coding must reduce infomation load sufficiently to permit retention; secondly it must ensure adequate connexions between codings and items so that retrieval is efficient. In both cases it is clear that efficiency of organisation at input should result in improved recall. If measures of organisation based on recall reflect organisation at input, then these measures should correlate with amount recalled. Failure to find a positive correlation may indicate that organisation of input is not efficient in the particular experimental situation. It does not indicate that subjects are incapable of organising efficiently at all.

b. *Evidence against a positive relationship*

There is a certain amount of evidence which indicates that the relationship between degree of organisation and amount recalled is less strong than the previous section suggests.

Firstly, the correlational evidence. While positive correlations between clustering and amount recalled are often evidenced over all subjects in an experiment, they are seldom found (or at least seldom reported) within groups. The same applies to differences between correlations for groups whose organisation differs as a result of independent variables. Furthermore, the correlation between ITR and amount recalled has not always been positive (18, 19). When subjects are divided into low, moderate, and high organisers, only the latter increased over trials both in ITR and in amount recalled (20, 21). It would seem that increased recall only results when degree of organisation is near optimal.

Secondly, there is the possibility that the positive correlations obtained are partly artefactual. Some measures of organisation habitually employed (see Appendix 1) have not been statistically independent of amount recalled. For example, a sequence of six items, three from one category followed by three from another, would have a lower clustering score than a sequence of nine items, three successively from each of three categories. The same is true of the ITR measure. Thus the measures result in the *amount recalled* placing an upper limit on the clustering score possible. However, when degree of organisation obtained is expressed as a percentage of the maximum organisation possible in that particular recall trial, statistical independence is assured.

Finally, there is the evidence of an important experiment by Puff (22). He divided subjects into clusterers and non-clusterers, defining a clusterer as any subject whose clustering was significantly above chance at a .05 level of probability. No difference in amount recalled was discovered between the two groups. However it should be stressed that the group of "clusterers" included both low and high clusterers; for if low and high clustering were to be defined in terms of percentage of the maximum clustering possible, the group would span a wide range. In another study, when the 18 highest and 18 lowest clusterers of 60 subjects were compared, it was found that the highest clusterers *did* recall more items (23). Moreover, Puff employed 30 items in three categories only; the storage and retrieval of ten items per coding throws such a heavy load on retrieval that categorical organisation might not be a worthwhile strategy in this case. Other organisation might have been employed which was not measured by the clustering measure. Thus Puff has not shown organisation and amount recalled to be unrelated; there is still the possiblity however, that only a high degree of organisation results in an increase in amount recalled.

c. *Conclusions*

It is clear that degree of organisation is very often positively related to amount recalled. It is also clear why such a relationship should theoretically be expected. What remains to be explained is why organisation is not used to its full potential.

The first possible explanation has already been proposed in the first section of this chapter. It is, briefly, that while subjects are potentially capable of coding input satisfactorily, they seldom have the time to do so. Presentation time may be limited, items numerous, and categories apparently unrelated. As a result, selection of codings is inappropriate, so that the item – coding relations are not strong enough and *retrieval* of items is poor. Or else coding of codings is inadequate, so that several codings are not *retained*, and whole groups or categories of items are lost. The specific experimental situation has limited the subject's potential organising capacity.

The second possible explanation concerns the nature of the measures of organisation (see Appendix 1). Degree of organisation is evidenced by the ordering of items in recall. Several measures do not index ordering alone; they allot a higher score for perfect ordering of a large number of items than for that of a smaller number. Other measures, however, would assess degree of organisation as 100% in both cases. They would deal with ordering alone. When the latter type of measure is employed, one might expect a lower degree of correlation. This is not only because of the danger of artefact in the case of the fonner type of measure. It is also because different variables might be involved. If different variables affect amount recalled and the percentage measures of organisation, then one would expect the correlation between the two to be lower.

Specifically, the degree of efficiency of coding would not affect ordering of items so much as amount recalled. Categories could be lost because of inadequate codings; items within categories could be lost because of poor selection of codings so that the coding – item relations were not strong enough. In both cases, amount recalled would suffer. However, ordering need not suffer, since although only 3 out of 5 categories, and 3 out of 5 items per category might be recalled, they could still be recalled in perfect categorical order.

Moreover, efficient ordering seems to require continue and stop rules. The subject needs to continue retrieving items by means of a coding until he has exhausted all the available presented items which that coding subsumes. Then he must apply a stop rule; he must cease generating items by means of the coding, put it aside, and start using another coding. These stop rules must also contain a check on whether the item has already been recalled or not, to avoid needless repetition. Rules of this sort imply continuous feedback during recall; they also imply the continuous availability of codings during recall.

There are, then, different variables affecting amount recalled and measures of organisation when these measures relate to ordering independent of amount recalled. Therefore we would not expect the correlation to be optimal. To summarise: if one defines degree of organisation strictly in terms of recall-independent measures, it is not highly related to amount recalled. If, however, we use measures of organisation which take efficiency of coding into account, the evidence indicates a very strong relationship.

References

1. MANDLER, G. (1966). 'Organisation and memory.' In K.W. SPENCE and J.T. SPENCE (Eds.) *The Psychology of Learning and Memory*. New York, Academic Press.
2. BOWER, G. (1969). 'Chunks as interference units in free recall.' *Journal of Verbal Learning and Verbal Behavior*, **8**, 610-613.
3. WEIST, R.M. (1970). 'Optimal versus non-optimal conditions for retrieval.' *Journal of Verbal Learning and Verbal Behavior*, **9**, 311-316.
4. EARHARD, M. (1967). 'Cued recall and free recall as a function of the number of items per cue.' *Journal of Verbal Learning and Verbal Behavior*, **6**, 257-263.
5. TULVING, E. (1962). 'Subjective organisation in free recall of "unrelated" words.' *Psychological Review*, **69**, 344-354.
6. SHAPIRO, S.I. and PONCE, I. (1970). 'Free recall and organisation as functions of paces or unpaced responding and presentation rate.' *Psychonomic Science*, **18**, 329-334.
7. TULVING, E. and PEARLSTONE, Z. (1966). 'Availability versus accessibility of information in memory for words.' *Journal of Verbal Learning and Verbal Behavior*, **5**, 381-391.
8. WOOD, G. (1967). 'Category names as cues for the recall of category instances.' *Psychonomic Science*, **9**, 323-324.
9. BAHRICK, H.P. (1971). 'Accessibility and availability of retrieval cues in the retention of a categorised list.' *Journal of Experimental Psychology*, **89**, 117-125.
10. CROUSE, J.H. (1968). 'Storage and retrieval of words in free-recall learning.' *Journal of Educational Psychology*, **59**, 449-451.
11. EARHARD, M. (1969). 'Storage and retrieval of words encoded in memory.' *Journal of Experimental Psychology*, **80**, 412-418.
12. HUDSON, R.L. (1969). 'Category clustering for immediate and delayed recall as a function of recall cue information and response dominance variability.' *Journal of Experimental Psychology*, **82**, 375-377.

13. HUDSON, R.L. and REYNOLDS, E.J. (1970). 'The effect on word recall when storage and retrieval cues differ.' *Psychonomic Science,* **4**, 211-216.
14. DONALDSON, W. (1971). 'Output effects in multitrial free recall.' *Journal of Verbal Learning and Verbal Behavior,* **10**, 577-582.
15. KINTSCH, W. (1968). 'Recognition and free recall of organised lists.' *Journal of Experimental Psychology,* **78**, 481-487.
16. HOGAN, R.M. and KINTSCH, W. (1971). 'Differential effects of study and test trials on long-term recognition and recall.' *Journal of Verbal Learning and Verbal Behavior,* **10**, 562-567.
17. MANDLER, G., PEARLSTONE, Z., and KOOPMANS, H.S. (1969). 'Effects of organisation and semantic similarity on recall and recognition.' *Journal of Verbal Learning and Verbal Behavior,* **8**, 410-423.
18. PUFF, C.R. (1970). 'Free recall with instructional manipulation of sequential ordering of output.' *Journal of Experimental Psychology,* **84**, 540-542.
19. POSTMAN, L. (1970). 'Effects of word frequency on acquisition and retention under conditions of free-recall learning.' *Quarterly Journal of Experimental Psychology,* **22**, 185-195.
20. SHAPIRO, S.I. and BELL, J.A. (1970). 'Subjective organisation and free recall: performance of high, moderate, and low organisers.' *Psychonomic Science,* **21**, 71-72.
21. EARHARD, M. and ENDICOTT, O. (1969). 'Why are there individual differences in subjective organisation during free recall memorisation?' *Journal of Verbal Learning and Verbal Behavior,* **8**, 316-318.
22. PUFF, C.R. (1970). 'Role of clustering in free recall.' *Journal of Experimental Psychology,* **86**, 384-386.
23. THOMPSON, C.P., HAMLIN, V.J., and ROENKER, D.L. (1972). 'A comment on the role of clustering in free recall.' *Journal of Experimental Psychology,* **94**, 108-109.

Chapter 4

The development of organised memory

a. Basic questions

The usefulness of the concept of process as an explanatory device will by now have become apparent. A process has been defined (see p. 3) as a series of events which forms an entity. Processes are inferred on the basis of a satisfactory amount of experimental evidence. Suppose a group of subjects are successful at an experimental task designed to evidence a process; the experimenter is apt to infer that the process is in existence, since he thinks it is available at least for that task in particular. Suppose, on the other hand, that a group of subjects either fails a task absolutely or relative to another group. One inference that is often made is that the process which the task is designed to evidence is not available at all to these subjects, or is only available in an impaired form. Another frequent inference is that the absence of the process in this particular task is due to features of the task which require other processes in addition (1). Thus an interaction of processes is required of the subject of which he may be incapable, although he may be perfectly capable of employing these processes individually in different circumstances. A final inference from failure at a task when similar tasks have been successfully accomplished previously is that this task requires a different process.

It is the writers' orientation to maintain that it is never in principle possible to assert that a process is absent. For there may be experimental tasks as yet not devised which might evidence its existence. Thus the onus is on the experimenter to devise means of experimentation which reveal the existence of processes. On the other hand, it is certainly not possible to maintain that all processes are potentially available in all subjects, and that they merely need an imaginative experimenter to reveal their existence. Although he may not infer absence of process, nevertheless the experimenter has an obligation to explain a failure to obtain a predicted result. He has to isolate those variables which have resulted in this failure; he has to identify the processes reflected by these variables and he has to explain why they should result in the absence of evidence of the process in which the experimenter is interested. If this explanation is not forthcoming, the failure to obtain the predicted effect puts at risk the very inference of the process itself. Indeed, it may then become necessary to infer a new process. Thus while failure to obtain the predicted evidence of a process cannot be taken as evidence of its absence or malfunction, this failure nevertheless has to be adequately explained in terms of other known processes also involved in the task.

Thus absolute or relative failure at a task does not necessarily evidence absence of process. Success, on the other hand, need not necessarily evidence its existence. Before the availability of a process to solve a task (and hence its existence) can be inferred, it has to be shown that the successful performance of the task in question requires the use of that process. The criterion for inferring that one process rather than another is being employed is that some independent variables, e.g., a, b, c, affect certain dependent variables, whereas others, e.g. x, y, z, do not. There are other tasks, on the other hand, in which the dependent variables are affected by x, y, z but not by a, b, c. Such qualitative differences permit the inference of different processes underlying the behaviours measured by the dependent variables.

There is, therefore, an obligation to evidence the availability of process for use in several tasks. For if its availability for only one type of task is 'evidenced', it is conceivable that the task in question requires a combination of so many different processes that the process which is assumed to be involved is not in fact necessary for its performance. Thus the experimenter has to show that success in obtaining the predicted effects is the result of the process in question; he will only do so by showing that the independent variables which have the predicted effects have the same effects when different task and dependent variables are introduced.

A further obligation upon the experimenter is to show that the independent variables he manipulates do not so alter the nature of the task that different processes are involved. For example, he has to show that his intervention in the free recall task does not perform the task for the subject so that secondary process is not required.

Finally, the experimenter has to be limited in the scope of his conclusions. Provided he has fulfilled the obligations outlined above, he can still only infer that a process is in existence and is available for use in the type(s) of experimental task which he has employed. He cannot infer that it is available for other tasks; for other tasks may involve additional processes, the limitations of which might prevent the use by the subject of the process in question. Generalisation and transfer must be evidenced in their own right.

There appear to be two basic experimental approaches within the area of developmental psychology. One is to present experimental tasks which have been employed to evidence processes in adult subjects. However, no assumptions are made that the performance of the task by children will require the inference of those same processes. The other is to assume that certain processes should be available, and then employ as many tasks as possible in an effort to infer their presence. The former makes fewer assumptions that children should employ the same processes as adults. The latter seems more likely to lead to the inference of deficiency, since repeated failure to obtain the predicted result has to be explained.

Both approaches nevertheless meet the difficulties outlined above. For both involve the inference of process from performance, and therefore incur the obligations which such an inference entails. Both, to differing degrees, run the risk of inferring that a process does not exist. This risk is particularly large in the case of children. For children may employ qualitatively different processes or different combinations of processes from adults. If he infers process from performance, the experimenter may be mistaken in assuming that the performance requires the same process in children as he supposes it requires in adults. If he infers absence of process, he makes the same assumption. The task may require other processes in addition to the process in question. These other processes might be more available to adults than to children, with the result that children fail the task. The experimenter is then in danger of assuming that the process in question is not even potentially available since the same task has suggested its existence in the case of adults. In fact, the children's failure is an artefact of the task; other processes have confounded results. Much of the most valuable recent research in developmental psychology has discovered new techniques which suggest that certain processes are potentially available at earlier ages than hitherto supposed (2).

The development of organised memory is an area of research which exemplifies the difficulties outlined above. The debate concerns whether children's performance on the free recall task requires the inference of secondary process; and whether other tasks might be used which reveal the existence of secondary process earlier in development than has so far been thought likely. One must ask what is the nature of the evidence required before the inference of secondary process can be made. The finding that significant clustering occurs may not be adequate evidence, since clustering need not necessarily require hierarchical coding processes. If secondary process is defined in terms of the coding of relations to reduce information load, then clearly it is not evidenced by significant clustering scores alone. Positive relations between degree of clustering and amount recalled would, on the other hand, tend to support the inference of secondary process; so would positive effects on amount recalled of certain forms of experimenter intervention. Finally, before the inference of secondary process can be made with any degree of confidence, tasks and material of different types must be employed.

b. The evidence

All experiments known to the writers have shown an increase in amount recalled with age. This increase appears to be present consistently when any age levels are compared. It applies to both categorisable (e.g. 3,4,5) and 'unrelated' (e.g. 6,7) items. However, the same is not true of organisation. In this case a sudden increase seems to occur at around CA 9 or 10 after a consistently low level up till that age.

Considering clustering first, studies using a recall-dependent measure found CA $4 < 9$ (5), and CA $9 < 12 < 21$ (8). Studies using a recall-independent measure found CA $6 = 9 < 14$ and CA $9 < 12$ (9); CA $5 = 7 = 9 < 11$ (10); and CA $9 < 21$ (11). Since amount recalled increases regularly with age, the recall-dependent measures may be artefactually contaminated. Nevertheless, an increase seems to occur around CA 9, although clustering even then is only around 40% of maximum possible.

Three experiments employing recall-independent measures find no age effect, however. The first (12) dealt with ages CA 3, 4, 5, 6 and 7, and therefore does not argue against the finding of an increase at CA 9. Nor does the second (13) which failed to find an increase between CA 5 and 8. The third (14) found no increase in all ages from CA 4 to 13 inclusive. However, there were only 4 categorically related items within an eight word list, with the result that the range of clustering scores possible was only 0 to 0.45. Moreover, only 4 subjects were employed at each age level.

The same conclusion may be drawn from research applying the ITR measure to 'unrelated' items. One experiment (15) shows an increase CA $6 < 11 < 14$, another (7) CA $9 < 12$, and a third (16) CA $5 = 8$. In all cases, only a very small percentage of total possible ITR occurs.

Indeed, it must be stressed that although measures of organisation are reported for very young children (e.g. 17), there is little evidence provided that the obtained organisation is significantly above chance; it is always a very small percentage of the total organisation possible, given the subject's recall; and it certainly need not be taken to indicate the existence of hierarchical processes involving coding of relations.

Evidence linking degree of organisation with amount recalled would support the postulation of hierarchical processes. However, once again such evidence is hard to find. One would expect independent variables concerned with organisation to increase amount recalled; and one would expect positive correlations between degree of organisation and amount recalled (see p. 22). Taking first the effect of independent variables upon recall; the only interaction effect of conditions with age upon recall known to the writers is the experiment of Lange and Hultsch (3). They found that the opportunity to actively sort the material resulted in increased recall only at CA 6-11, not CA 13 or 15. Other experiments which find condition x age interactions on clustering (5,10) do not find similar effects on recall. Significant correlations between degree of organisation and amount recalled are likewise hard to find. One experiment (7) finds a positive correlation between ITR and amount recalled at CA 10, but not at CA 8. However, this correlation is not consistent over days, occurring on only three of four experimental sessions. Thus what evidence there is suggests that organisation does not result in an increase in amount recalled until the age of CA 9 or 10. Perhaps the low organisation scores achieved at younger ages might be due to other processes, such as, for example, sequential processes in which each item cued the next as a result of inter-item association.

In summary, the evidence shows that

(a) Amount recalled increases steadily with age.

(b) An increase from a low to a moderate degree of clustering occurs around CA 9 or 10.

(c) There is little evidence for a relation between degree of organisation and amount recalled. What evidence there is suggests that this relationship may obtain at around the same age.

c. *Theoretical considerations*

Any explanation of these results must take into account general features of cognitive development. It is possible that the perfect or near perfect ordering of recall and the use of such organisation to increase amount recalled require hierarchical processes (see p. 22). That is, they require the use of superordinate tags to store and retrieve by, which permits reduction of information and hence increased recall. These hierarchical processes are also exemplified in the class inclusion operation postulated by Piaget. This operation requires subordinates, superordinates and the relations between them to be held in mind. Such an operation is considered typical of the child who has reached the stage of concrete operational thinking. For it not only requires the internalisation of actions but also their manipulation in hierarchical ways.

The evidence that only children of what is generally considered to be a well developed operational age (CA 9-10) can recall with a moderate degree of organisation and use such organisation to increase amount recalled suggests that operational thinking is required to ensure these results. Only two reports known to the authors have specifically stated these hypotheses (18,19). Unfortunately, in one case (18) the results are inconclusive as there was not a wide enough age range employed, and as the sex variable confounded developmental predictions. In the other case (19) the material consisted of unrelated items. However, this latter experiment discovered that in terms of amount recalled, degree of organisation, and efficiency of sorting, CA $6 = 8 < 10 = 12$. It also found that there was no correlation between degree of organisation and amount recalled until CA 12.

If the Piagetian interpretation is justified, then the hierarchical processes involved in the coding of relations and their use for storage and retrieval of items are dependent upon the child's attainment of the stage of operational thinking. However, certain reservations must be made.

Firstly, the attainment of operational thinking is not tied to a fixed chronological age. Recent experiments (2) have shown that one can never maintain confidently that operational thinking is not available to children of a certain age. Thus if operational thinking *is* a necessary condition for hierarchical processes in memory, this does not mean that hierarchical processes cannot appear before a certain age.

Indeed, one particular hypothesis advanced by Flavell (et al) (20,21), suggests that it is only inability to apply organisation to input spontaneously ('production deficiency') which prevents the use of mediational processes by much younger children. Flavell and his associates maintain that even children of CA 5 are capable of employing mediators to aid their recall. Unfortunately, they use the absence of a conditions x age interaction effect upon amount recalled, but its presence upon clustering, to support their case (10). It has been consistently proposed in this book that effects of independent variables upon amount recalled have to be evidenced before the use of hierarchical processes can be postulated with confidence.

Secondly, the age of 9 to 10 at which increased organisation and its effect upon amount recalled are first recorded has no great significance. The material employed has consisted of culturally determined semantic categories, but this need not be an essential feature of the evidence for hierarchical processes. Indeed, it is possible that the coding of relations between items could occur much earlier if the relations concerned were not so culturally determined. If, for example, the basis of the relations was more relevant to the child's experience than semantic categories, the use of superordinate codings of items might possibly occur at a younger age. However, it is difficult to imagine the type of material or experimental situation which could provide such evidence.

Thus the development of organisation and its use to aid recall seems to be closely tied to overall cognitive development. However, the steady increase in amount recalled per se does not require or permit the same explanation. Other processes might well develop steadily with age. Older subjects may be capable of rehearsing more, and may employ the strategy of rehearsal to increase the amount they recall (22). Also, their coding *of items* may become more efficient.

The development of secondary process in normal children has clear connexions with the area of subnormality. In both cases the stage of cognitive development attained may be crucial; the need to evidence hierarchical processes is vital; and the danger of inferring absence of process is considerable.

References

1. COLE, M. and BRUNER, J.S. (1971). 'Cultural differences and inferences about psychological processes.' *American Psychologist*, **26**, 867-876.
2. BRYANT, P.E. (1971). 'Cognitive development.' *British Medical Bulletin*, 27. 200-205.
3. LANGE, G.W. and HULTSCH, D.F. (1970). 'The development of free classification and free recall in children.' *Developmental Psychology*, **3**, 408-415.
4. WACHS, T.D. (1969). 'Free recall learning in children as a function of CA, IQ, and motivational orientation.' *Child*

Development, **40**, 577-589.

5. YOSHIMURA, E.K., MOELY, B.E., and SHAPIRO, S.I. (1971). 'The influence of age and presentation order upon children's free recall and learning to learn.' *Psychonomic Science*, **23**, 261-263.
6. LAWRENCE, M.W. (1966). 'Age differences in performance and subjective organisation in the free-recall learning of pictorial material.' *Canadian Journal of Psychology*, **20**, 388-399.
7. SHAPIRO, S.I. and MOELY, B.E. (1971). 'Free recall, subjective organisation, and learning to learn at three age levels.' *Psychonomic Science*, **23**, 189-190.
8. GERJUOY, I.R. and SPITZ, H.H. (1966). 'Associative clustering in free recall: intellectual and developmental variables.' *American Journal of Mental Deficiency*, **70**, 918-927.
9. COLE, M., FRANKEL, F., and SHARP, D. 'Development of free recall learning in children.' *Developmental Psychology*, **4**, 109-123.
10. MOELY, B.E., OLSON, F.A., HALWES, T.G., and FLAVELL, J.H., (1969). 'Production deficiency in young children's clustered recall'. *Developmental Psychology*, **1**, 16-34.
11. BOUSFIELD, W.A., ESTERSON, J., and WHITMARSH, G.A. (1958). 'A study of developmental changes in conceptual and perceptual associative clustering.' *Journal of Genetic Psychology*, **92**, 95-102.
12. MOELY, B.E. and SHAPIRO, S.I. (1971). 'Free recall and clustering at four age levels: Effects of learning to learn and presentation method.' *Developmental Psychology*, **4**, 490.
13. HOROWITZ, A.B. (1969). 'Effects of stimulus presentation modes on children's recall and clustering.' *Psychonomic Science*, **14**, 297-298.
14. STEINMETZ, J.I. and BATTIG, W.F. (1969). 'Clustering and priority in free recall of newly learned items in children.' *Developmental Psychology*, **1**, 503-507.
15. ROSNER, S.R. (1971). 'The effects of rehearsal and chunking instructions on children's multi-trial free recall.' *Journal of Experimental Child Psychology*, **11**, 93-105.
16. NELSON, K.J. (1969). 'The organisation of free-recall by young children.' *Journal of Experimental Child Psychology*, **8**, 284-296.

17. ROSSI, S. and WITTROCK, M.C. (1971). 'Developmental shifts in verbal recall between mental age two and five.' *Child Development*, 42, 333-338.
18. OLSON, D.R. and CROSBIE, D. (1971). 'Does the structure of verbal memory change with the onset of concrete operations?' (in preparation).
19. MANDLER, G., and STEPHENSON, D. (1967). 'The development of free and constrained conceptualisation and subsequent verbal memory.' *Journal of Experimental Child Psychology*, 5, 86-93.
20. FLAVELL, J.H., BEACH, D.H., and CHINSKY, J.M. (1966). 'Spontaneous verbal rehearsal in a memory task as a function of age.' *Child Development*, 37, 283-299.
21. KEENEY, T.J., CANNIZZO, S.R., and FLAVELL, J.H. (1967). 'Spontaneous and induced verbal rehearsal in a recall task.' *Child Development*, 38, 953-966.
22. BELMONT, J.M. and BUTTERFIELD, E.C. (1969). 'The relations of short-term memory to development and intelligence.' In LIPSITT, L.P. & REESE, H.W. (Eds.) *Advances in Child Development and Behavior*. Vol. 4. New York, Academic Press.

Part Two

Organisation and memory in the subnormal

Chapter 5

Previous research

a. Methodology of subnormality research

The experimental approach to the area of memory in normal subjects has resulted in the inference of secondary processes described in the previous four chapters. Exactly the same approach appears to be profitable in the case of the subnormal (1); just as normal children have been presented with free recall tasks in an effort to discover which processes could be inferred from their performance, so subnormals may be presented with the same tasks. However, just as caution needed to be exercised concerning the inference of presence or absence of processes in children, so it does with subnormals. In particular, caution is required regarding the inference of absence of or defect in a process (27). The possibility has to be taken into account that because of some overall feature of their information processing system (e.g. low overall capacity) the specific experimental task does not permit them to use a process which they have potentially available. Or it may be that they use different processes from normal adults in experimental tasks.

Unfortunately, workers in the field have tended to ignore this overall research strategy. Instead of treating the subnormal as a population in their own right, they have employed control groups of normal subjects so that comparisons between normals and subnormals may be made (2). Their purpose is to detail the differences between normals and subnormals rather than to discover which processes need to be postulated to account for subnormals' performance at certain tasks.

There are, however, certain fundamental difficulties in the use of normal controls, even granted that they appear necessary if the experimenter's objective is comparison (3). Firstly, consider the use of normal MA controls. In this case the control group consists of normal children who are of the same MA as the subnormals. Thus one might have, for example, a group or groups of subnormals of CA 15 and MA 7 being compared with a group or groups of normals of CA and MA 7. The subnormals are usually drawn from one type of institution, and are then further selected as the result of their performance on a test of 'general intelligence'; their level of ability is sometimes expressed as an IQ but more usually as an MA.

In the use of MA controls, the intelligence test is being used as an index of level of cognitive development. Comparison implies that differences may be discovered between the subnormal and normals at the same level of development. Cogent criticisms of this use of intelligence tests may be made. Firstly, such tests seldom take account of what is known about cognitive development, and the vastly different life experiences of subnormals aged from 10 to 25 and normals aged from 4 to 8 make their interpretation very difficult. In particular, the same overall global measure of MA might be derived from vastly different profiles of performance on subtests.

Furthermore, if standard tests of intelligence are used as indices of cognitive development and ever more sophisticated experimental procedures are designed to test specific functions, then inevitably the difference in sensitivity of measurement will result in artefactual differences between subnormals and MA controls. To employ a reductio ad absurdum, if the ultimate intelligence test were to be created and used for purposes of selection of subjects, then any difference between those subjects obtained in an experiment would have to be considered as evidence that the groups were not properly matched in the first instance! In brief, if the test is an imperfect form of control, then differences found by experiment can be attributed to these imperfections; if it is a perfect form of control there should be no experimental differences.

It is also worth noting that if the test of intelligence is taken as an index of general cognitive development; if the groups are to be considered matched; and if specific experimental procedures are taken as indices of particular abilities; then it follows that a roughly equal number of abilities should be superior as are inferior. Few such findings have been reported.

Finally, there are considerable methodological difficulties in setting up experiments using normal controls (3). In particular, floor and ceiling effects are likely to operate (4), especially when experimenter intervention occurs. Thus, for example, if a group of CA normal controls on a no cue condition in a free recall experiment scores higher than the subnormal group, their performance when provided with cues might not show so much of an improvement; firstly, because they start from a higher baseline comparison, and secondly because they might approach the ceiling performance on the task in question.

As a result of the use of normal controls, certain theoretical controversies have occupied the time of several of the foremost workers in the field. In particular, defect and developmental theorists have regarded their positions as mutually exclusive (5). If differences are found between subnormals and MA controls on experimental tasks, defect theorists suppose that the subnormals have defects in the processes required for those tasks. These specific defects have been postulated to account for poor cognitive functioning. Developmentalists point to the many experiments which fail to find consistent differences; further, they endeavour to explain those differences which are found in terms of such features as different degrees of social reinforcement experienced by the two groups (5). Clearly, this controversy depends for its existence upon the use of MA controls as a comparison group in terms of general developmental level.

Another form of comparison is with CA rather than MA controls. That is, subnormals of, for example, CA 15 and MA 7 might be compared with normals of CA (and by implication, MA) 15. Clearly, one would predict that in most experimental tasks, the subnormal group would be inferior to the control group, since the criterion for their selection was inferior performance on a test of "general intelligence". Since these tests require a considerable range of skills, it is reasonable to predict that the skill sampled by the experimental task was also required to a greater or lesser extent in the test of intelligence. However, there are occasions when the subnormal group is not inferior to the controls (4); this argues the possibility of different profiles of specific abilities as opposed to different levels of general ability. However, at least the CA matching procedure only requires the use of the intelligence test as a criterion for the selection of subjects; the MA match, by comparison, requires its use as an index of cognitive development.

Normal control groups have therefore been discarded in the research project to be described in subsequent chapters. Firstly, because the objective is not to compare subnormals with normals. Rather, following the lead of other experimenters (e.g. 6, 7 and 8) it is to discover what processes they have available. Secondly, normal control groups have not been used because of the cogent objections to their use outlined above. Thirdly, they have not been used because they lead to a defect orientation. Any comparison with normals is bound to focus attention on supposed deficiencies, and it has been stressed throughout that it is notoriously difficult to infer absence or impairment of a process.

It may nevertheless be objected that any research on subnormals uses normal controls implicitly. While this is clearly true in terms of the selection of subjects, it need not be true in terms of the inferences one draws from experimental results. The task may differ in difficulty or indeed in nature from tasks employed with normals, and different processes may be evidenced. No direct comparison between normal and subnormal is intended. Nevertheless it would be theoretically interesting and practically important to discover that the same processes have to be postulated to account for the behaviour of subnormals as for normals.

The major difficulty facing any experimenter employing the above strategy with subnormals is that of the immense inter-subject variability typical of these subjects. Any experimenter intervention may be ineffective as a result of inter-subject variance. If the experimenter's objective is to make generalisations about as wide a range of subnormals as possible, he will be running this risk. He will also run the risk of considering as a single population what might turn out to be several populations from a psychological point of view. If, however, he wishes to explore the sources of variance and control them experimentally, he may obtain more detailed findings; but these may be applicable to a smaller population only. Perhaps a good strategy is to move from wider to more defined populations; for the experimental investigation of the former might result in the discovery of the significant parameters which distinguish sub-populations.

Apart from this strategical choice, the selection of criterion measures by which to equate experimental treatment groups of subnormals is a major methodological difficulty. One solution has been to equate on a task resembling the experimental task itself.

b. Input organisation deficiency

The major work on secondary processes in the subnormal has been carried out by Gerjuoy, Spitz, and their associates. Although they have operated with a defect orientation, their thorough work provides the basis for what is known.

Research prior to their work is summarised by Blount (9) and Spitz (10). Generalisations are hazardous, as inadequate measures of clustering, different types of matching to control groups, and different types of material presented in different modalities were employed. In general, organisation was found in subnormals' recall (11, 12, 13). In some cases, they displayed less clustering than MA (13) and CA (14) controls, but in another case the MA finding was not repeated (12). No significant differences were found between aetiological subgroups (11) or between groups of different levels of intelligence (15). Increase in clustering over trials was found (13). Thus early studies suggested that, given favourable circumstances such as visual (11) or bi-modal (12) presentation, clustering could occur. But they suggested the possibility that subnormals clustered less than MA controls; and they universally found that they were worse at clustering than CA controls. In all cases where CA controls were used, the recall of the subnormals was inferior.

The body of research initiated by Gerjuoy and Spitz (16) employed both CA and MA controls. However, the control subjects were only employed in the random-order control condition. Presentation was auditory and sequential for their multi-trial task, with the material consisting of 20 items, 5 each from 4 categories. They employed 4 conditions – a random order no cues condition; a blocked presentation condition in which items from the same category were presented in sequence (but with a different sequence of items within categories and of categories themselves on each trial); a requested clustered condition, in which subjects were asked during recall to remember items in response to category labels, e.g. 'What animals were there?'; and a presented blocked plus requested clustered condition.

In terms of both clustering (O-E) and amount recalled, the subnormal subjects were inferior to the CA but not to the MA controls. Moreover, as in the case of other experiments (17, 18), blocked presentation resulted in increased clustering over the random order condition. The requested clustered condition also resulted in increased recall, being equally as effective as the blocked presentation condition. No results are presented for clustering in the two requested clustered conditions. The presented blocked plus requested clustered condition was superior to both these conditions singly in terms of amount recalled. The only evidence of a positive correlation between clustering and amount recalled was for one trial in the blocked presentation condition.

Gerjuoy and Spitz interpret these results in terms of input deficiency. That is, they consider firstly the fact that there was no significant difference between obtained and expected by chance clustering on the random order control condition for subnormals; secondly, the fact that blocked presentation did result in such a difference; and they infer that these results support Spitz's theory of a general deficiency of organisation at input (10). As has been suggested, however, absence of a significant difference between obtained and expected clustering might be due to specific features of this task, for example, the identity of the categories and items, and the sequential auditory mode of presentation. Nevertheless, it must be emphasised that Spitz produces evidence from other areas of research to support his general theory. O'Connor and Hermelin (19) provide much more evidence along these lines.

Explanation of the various conditions effects is difficult. The blocked presentation condition may have resulted, by its juxtaposition of related items, in drawing subjects' attention to the relations between them. They might then have coded these relations and employed them successfully to increase amount recall and clustering. Alternatively, blocked presentation may lead to a sequential strategy whereby each item cues the next in a sequence. This could result from previously existing inter-item associations being activated by the near juxtaposition of categorically related items; for the categorically related items appear likely to be highly associatively related also. It is easy to see how this strategy could lead to increased clustering in recall and to elucidate why it should result in greater amount recalled.

The requested clustered condition likewise resulted in increased recall over the no cues condition; clustering also probably increased, although this is not reported. Here, too, difficulties in interpretation arise. One explanation for increased recall could be that more categories (as opposed to more items per category) were recalled, since the category labels were provided at recall. However, only four categories were employed in this task. Perhaps a more plausible explanation is that when given category labels, subjects used them to generate all the appropriate items they could think of. Items which were not among those presented would in this case be screened out by a recognition check (20). Such a recognition check would be under a lot of pressure, since many items might be generated which were not presented. This overloading would therefore be expected to result in a higher rate of intrusions in recall of categorically related items, and indeed, Gerjuoy and Spitz report that this occurred. A final possible explanation for the effect of the requested clustered condition is that subjects supplied their own codings at presentation and that these were reinstated by the cues at recall; the identity of presentation and recall codings would then result in the reduction of information load, since codings, not items, were retained.

This latter explanation might also be appropriate in the case of the presented blocked plus requested clustered condition, in which amount recalled exceeded its two constituent conditions. It might be supposed that the blocked presentation led to the application of codings while cues reinstated them at recall, thereby making them immediately available for retrieval purposes. Furthermore, since a multi-trial situation was employed, the recall cues could be applied by subjects at the next presentation trial. On the other hand, the alternative explanations suggested above in the case of the constituent conditions may also be applicable here. That is, the blocked presentation constituent resulted in categorically related items cueing each other in sequence; the requested clustered condition resulted in the generation of items from the appropriate category.

Thus the results of Gerjuoy and Spitz are very important, in that the interventions they employed facilitated clustering and recall.

c. *Modality and transfer effects*

Gerjuoy, Winters, Pullen and Spitz (21) employed visual rather than auditory presentation. Presentation was of item by item consecutively, however, rather than of all items simultaneously. They failed to find any differences in amount recalled due to blocked presentation but did find such an effect on clustering (O-E). Moreover, MA controls were found to cluster more than the subnormals. Gerjuoy (et al) compared their results with those of Gerjuoy and Spitz (16). They found that random order visual presentation led to better recall than the random order auditory presentation of Gerjouy and Spitz; but that the blocked presentation of auditory material in the earlier experiment led to greater recall than their own blocked presentation of visual material. However, comparison does not seem justified, since the items were of a very different type in the two experiments. Gerjuoy (et al) used such items as digits, shapes and colours, whereas Gerjuoy and Spitz had employed more orthodox semantic categories. Blocked presentation should help more with this latter type of material, since inter-item associations and codings are more likely to be available in the case of well-established semantic categories. Furthermore, the rate of presentation of items differed in the two experiments.

Gerjuoy and Winters (22) aimed to compare auditory plus visual (bi-modal) presentation with Gerjuoy and Spitz's findings (they had employed auditory presentation). They found that greater recall was obtained from the pooled results of their four bi-modal conditions than Gerjuoy and Spitz found in their blocked presentation condition and in their requested clustered condition. Gerjuoy and Winters' treatment groups varied along two dimensions. These were whether pictures where presented singly or in groups of five ('grouping'); and whether the list was in random order or categorically related items occurred adjacently (blocked presentation). These conditions had no differential effects on amount recalled. However, there was a main effect of blocked presentation on clustering, and also a blocking x grouping interaction. Using the same subjects one week later, Gerjuoy and Winters found greater recall of bi-modal over auditory presentation, but no effect of modality on clustering. Evans (23) also found the modality effect on recall but not on clustering.

Gerjuoy and Winters review the literature in terms of the relation between clustering and recall. They find that when presentation is auditory (16, 24), clustering *is* correlated with recall, and the same independent variables affect both clustering and amount recalled. However, when presentation is visual (21) or when it is bi-modal (22), blocked presentation increases clustering but not amount recalled. Gerjuoy and Winters conclude that presentation must be auditory for clustering and amount recalled to be related. They postulate different types of coding for the two modalities.

An important question concerns transfer. While clustering and recall may increase over trials in the multi-trial procedure (e.g. 22), little evidence is available that clustering or the use of clustering to aid recall transfers to different material. Bilsky and Evans (25) found that blocked presentation on the first two trials of a four-trial session led to more clustering on the randomly ordered second two trials than did random-order presentation of the first two trials. This only applied to the same items, however. It did not apply to different items from the same categories, let alone to different items from different categories (28). Reiss (26) found an increase over lists in recall, two out of the three of his lists being presented blocked. Gerjuoy and Alvarez (24) found no transfer from 5 trials of blocked auditory presentation to random order auditory presentation of different items from different categories one week later. That is, they failed to find significant differences on the test phase on day 2 between a group who had received blocked presentation and a control group who had received random order presentation in the training phase one week earlier on day 1. However, since blocked presentation may not make the organisational strategy clear to the subject, this result is perhaps not surprising.

Clarke, Clarke and Cooper (8) nevertheless did succeed in finding some transfer effect of auditory blocked presentation. Their training phase was very lengthy, being terminated either after 24 trials or after subjects had succeeded in recalling 15 out of 16 items on four consecutive trials. The transfer effect due to blocked presentation evidenced in amount recalled on the test phase only occurred on the first two trials of the test task. Clarke (et al) did employ another form of assistance; they instructed their subjects that the words belonged to categories and told them the category names. However, this did not increase recall over a random order condition on the training task, and thus stood no chance of resulting in transfer. In a subsequent attempt to elicit transfer from an auditory mode of training to a visual test, blocked presentation resulted in transfer only on the first recall trial. The relative success of Clarke (et al) as compared to Gerjuoy and Alvarez (24) may be attributed to their ensuring that subjects were more thoroughly trained.

One possible criticism of blocked presentation is that it may be specific to the material employed. Further, it gives insufficient help. It might be supposed that instructions to recall in an organised way (i.e. selection of organisational strategy for the subject); presentation and recall cues (i.e. provision of codings, their retention, and directions to use them for retrieval); or a combination of both these conditions would be more likely to lead to positive transfer. For the learning of strategies of organisation involves more than perception of relations; it requires mastery of the total process and its coherent use.

In summary, research with subnormal subjects indicates that it is possible that secondary processes are potentially available to subnormal subjects for use in the free recall situation; for there is some evidence that amount recalled as well as order of recall is affected by experimenter-provided assistance.

References

1. O'CONNOR, N. & HERMELIN, B. (1972). 'Cognitive deficits in children.' *British Medical Bulletin*, 27, 227-231.
2. HEAL, L.W. (1970). 'Research strategies and research goals in the scientific study of the mentally subnormal.' *American Journal of Mental Deficiency*, 75, 10-15.
3. BAUMEISTER, A.A. (1967). 'Problems in comparative studies of mental retardates and normals.' *American Journal of Mental Deficiency*, 71, 869-875.
4. BELMONT, J.M. & BUTTERFIELD, E.C. (1969). 'The relations of short-term memory to development and intelligence.'

In LIPSITT, L.P. & REESE, H.W. (Eds.) *Advances in Child Development and Behavior,* Vol. 4. New York, Academic Press.

5. ZIGLER, E (1969). 'Developmental versus difference theories of mental retardation and the problem of motivation.' *American Journal of Mental Deficiency,* 73, 536-556.

6. BAUMEISTER, A.A. & KELLAS, G. (1971). 'Process variables in the paired associate learning of retardates.' In ELLIS , N.R. (Ed.) *International Review of Research in Mental Retardation,* Vol. 5. New York, Academic Press.

7. CLARKE, A.M. & CLARKE, A.D.B. (1967). 'Learning transfer and cognitive development.' In ZUBIN, J. & JERVIS, G.A. (Eds.) *Psychopathology of Mental Development.* New York, Grune & Stratton.

8. CLARKE, A.M., CLARKE, A.D.B., & COOPER, G.M. (1970). 'The development of a set to perceive categorical relations.' In HAYWOOD, H.C. (Ed.) *Social-cultural Aspects of Mental Retardation.* New York, Appleton-Century-Crofts.

9. BLOUNT, W.R. (1968). 'Concept usage research with the mentally retarded.' *Psychological Bulletin,* 69, 281-294.

10 SPITZ, H.H. (1966). 'The role of input organisation in the learning and memory of mental retardates.' In ELLIS, N.R. (Ed.) *International Review of Research in Mental Retardation,* Vol. 2, New York, Academic Press.

11. WEATHERWAX, J. and BENOIT, E.P. (1957). 'Concrete and abstract thinking in organic and non-organic mentally retarded children.' *American Journal of Mental Deficiency,* 62, 548-553.

12. OSBORN, W.J. (1960). 'Associative clustering in organic and familial retardates.' *American Journal of Mental Deficiency,* 65, 351-357.

13. ROSSI, E.L. (1963). 'Associative clustering in normal and retarded children.' *American Journal of Mental Deficiency,* 67, 691-699.

14. STEDMAN, D.J. (1963). 'Associative clustering of semantic categories in normal and retarded subjects.' *American Journal of Mental Deficiency,* 67, 700-704.

15. EVANS, R.A. (1964). 'Word recall and associative clustering in mental retardates.' *American Journal of Mental Deficiency,* 69, 413-418.

16. GERJUOY, I.R. and SPITZ, H.H. (1966). 'Associative clustering in free recall: Intellectual and developmental variables.'

American Journal of Mental Deficiency, **70**, 918-927.
17. REISS, P. and REISS, R. (1972). 'Clustering and subjective organisation in a free-recall task with retardates: A comparison of two methodologies.' *American Journal of Mental Deficiency* (in press).
18. SIMPSON, R.L., KING, J.D. and DREW, C.J. (1970). 'Free recall by retarded and non-retarded subjects as a function of input organisation.' *Psychonomic Science*, **19**, 334-338.
19. O'CONNOR, N. & HERMELIN, B. (1963). *Speech and Thought in Severe Subnormality*. Oxford, Pergamon Press.
20. KINTSCH, W. (1969). 'Models for free recall and recognition.' In NORMAN, D.A. (Ed.) *Models of Memory*. New York, Academic Press.
21. GERJUOY, I.R., WINTERS, J.J., PULLEN, M.M., & SPITZ, H.H. (1969). 'Subjective organisation by retardates and normals during free recall of visual stimuli.' *American Journal of Mental Deficiency*, **73**, 791-797.
22. GERJUOY, I.R. & WINTERS, J.J. (1970). 'Subjective organisation by EMR adolescents in free recall: bi-modal presentation.' *American Journal of Mental Deficiency*, **74**, 509-516.
23. EVANS, R.A. (1970). 'Use of associative clustering technique in the study of reading disability: effects of presentation mode.' *American Journal of Mental Deficiency*, **74**, 765-770.
24. GERJUOY, I.R. & ALVAREZ, J.M. (1969). 'Transfer of learning in associative clustering of retardates and normals during free recall of visual stimuli.' *American Journal of Mental Deficiency*, **73**, 791-797.
25. BILSKY, L. & EVANS, R.A. (1970). 'Use of associative clustering technique in the study of reading disability: effects of list organisation.' *American Journal of Mental Deficiency*, **74**, 771-776.
26. REISS, P. (1968). 'Rhyming and conceptual relationships in a free recall task with retardates.' *American Journal of Mental Deficiency*, **73**, 81-85.
27. BORTNER, M.A. & BIRCH, H.G. (1970). 'Cognitive capacity and cognitive competence.' *American Journal of Mental Deficiency*, **74**, 735-744.
28. BILSKY, L., EVANS, R.A. & GILBERT, H. (1972). 'Generalisation of associative clustering tendencies in mildly retarded adolescents: Effects of novel stimuli'. *American Journal of Mental Deficiency*, **77**, 77-84.

Chapter 6

Introduction to the project

a. Aims and objectives of the research

The overall aim of the research project to be described is to discover whether the same processes can be inferred to account for the free recall performance of subnormals as are hypothesised to account for that of normals. The specific population employed in the project consisted of adults attending adult day training centres (with the exception of two experiments). The average vocabulary age (VA) within each experiment as evidenced by the English Picture Vocabulary Test (EPVT) (1) (See Appendix 2) ranged from 5 to 8 years. The subjects used in the project were therefore less able performers on such a test than the subjects employed by other experimenters. In general, the MA or VA of their subjects ranged from 8 or 9 (e.g. 2) to 10 or 11 (e.g. 3). It was hoped that the potential of subnormal individuals of lower intelligence might be shown to be greater than hitherto recognised. Throughout the project, mongoloid and non-mongoloid individuals were considered separately, in an effort to discover whether aetiological variables are relevant to free-recall performance.

Provision by the experimenter of different types of assistance was the means by which the aims might be realised. It has been argued throughout this book that the basic purpose of such intervention is to demonstrate that processes are available. The type of assistance varies considerably. This is because it was aimed to show that different features of secondary processes were available. Previously, experimenter intervention in free recall by subnormals has largely been limited to the technique of blocked presentation. As has been suggested, this might result in learning by temporal contiguity and subsequent use of a sequential rather than an hierarchical strategy. Therefore in general modes of assistance were employed in the present project which were aimed at encouraging hierarchical strategies. That is, it was hoped to elicit the use of codings of relations for storage and retrieval, in an effort to discover whether organisation was positively related to amount recalled. The objective was therefore not merely to elicit organisation as evidenced by order of recall, but rather to elicit the use of organisation to aid amount recalled. A further objective was to see if transfer of this strategy to a similar unaided task could occur.

The project will be reported in a logical rather than a chronological order. The research will not be dealt with experiment by experiment so much as in terms of different aspects of secondary processes. Particular problems arise with regard to the level of detail employed in the reporting of procedures and results. We have decided to exclude detailed procedural matters from the text, but have included a table to which the reader may refer for further information. (Table 1, pp. 56-57).

b. General features of the experiments

Certain features common to most or all of the experiments will now be described.

With regard to *subjects,* these were selected and matched according to several criteria. Firstly, VA as measured by the EPVT (see Appendix 2). Secondly, the Basic Recall Ability Test (BRA) (employed in later experiments only). This consisted of 16 apparently unrelated items, which were presented for 80 seconds, and for the free recall of which the same period was allowed. Details of the test, its reliability, and its correlation with dependent variables, are presented in Appendix 3. Both in the case of BRA and of the actual experimental procedure, subjects were shown the items on a naming trial before the first presentation proper. If subjects even after instruction, could not name the BRA or experimental items, they were rejected. Grounds for selection or rejection were thus VA, BRA, and ability to name items. In addition to the requirements of equating treatment groups on these criteria, various lower and upper limits on VA (see Table 1) and a lower limit of 5 on BRA were set. Finally, wherever possible CA was also controlled across treatment groups. Approximately 550 individuals were employed as subjects of whom approximately 20% partook in more than one experiment. Apart from in Experiments 2 and 3, no subject was employed within a year of previous testing.

With regard to *experimental design and procedure,* all experiments except Experiment 4 used the free-recall technique and employed group designs. All subjects were tested individually, in a room apart from the room in which they were working. In all cases, at least two experimenters were employed, one dealing with the subject and the other manipulating the equipment. Within each experiment, the same experimenter dealt with all subjects on all sessions.

Presentation in every case was visual, items being presented simultaneously rather than successively, by means of Kodak Carousel slide projector (except in Experiments 9 and 10). The purpose of visual simultaneous presentation was to ensure that subjects had the opportunity to spot relations between items while these were all present.* The order of items within the array was random and different for each presentation trial. In every case, subjects were told before the first presentation trial that they would have to remember the items and tell the experimenter what they were after they had gone away.

Recall was always required immediately after presentation, although in effect the switching off of the slide projector and the request for recall occupied 2-3 seconds. Verbal praise was given intermittently during recall, and after periods of silence during the recall phase the subject was prompted by such phrases as 'Was there anything else?' or 'There was a ....(pause)'. Subjects were not criticised when they repeated items they had already recalled. However, the experimenter asked the subject to tell him items he had not told him already if repetitions became very numerous. In general, procedure was so designed as to optimise performance in organisation and recall without providing specific help (although of course in most cases additional specific help was provided).

EPVT and BRA were administered on a day prior to the experiment proper. When the experiment consisted of more than one session, sessions occurred on consecutive days, and always employed different material.

In terms of *analysis of results*, the basic statistic employed was analysis of variance. When further analysis of differences between groups within a factor was required, tests of the Newman-Keuls type (4) were employed. Correlation coefficients cited are Pearson's Product Moment unless otherwise stated. The dependent variables were amount recalled, expressed in terms of number of items correct, and degree of organisation. Several measures of organisation were applied (see Appendix 1). Results and analyses will not be treated in full. Tables or figures giving the main results for each experiment will be provided where necessary. However, details of analyses of variance will not be provided. Furthermore, in order to avoid punctuating the text with detailed probability levels, the following convention will be used. 'Just significant' will refer to $p < \cdot05$, 'significant' to $p < \cdot01$, and 'highly significant' to $p < \cdot005$ or better.

* See Postscript on page 58.

Table 1 *Experimental Details*

Experiment No.	*Factor 1*	*Factor 2*	*Factor 3*
1	Mongoloid v non-mongoloid	Expected v Obtained (Clustering & ITR)	–
2	Mongoloid v non-mongoloid	Labelling in recall order v in random order of unrelated items.	Days (2)
3	Mongoloid v non-mongoloid	Labelling in recall order v in random order of categorisable items.	Days (2)
4	Sorting experiment		
5	Mongoloid v non-mongoloid	No cues v miming cues v verbal cues v miming + verbal cues	Days (3)
6	No cues v presentation cues v recall cues v presentation + recall cues	Days (3)	Recall trials (2)
7	Lower VA v higher VA	Pres. + rec. cues v no cues	Trials (5)
8	Compatible v incompatible sets	No cues v presentation cues v recall cues v incompatible pres. + rec. cues v compatible pres. + recall cues	Trials (3)
9	Grouped v random presentation	Cues v no cues	Trials (5)
10	No instruction v fours v grouping v cues	Active v passive	Trials (5)
11	Instructions v no instructions	Pres. + rec. cues v no cues	Trials (5)
12	Mongoloid v non-mongoloid	Pres. + rec. cues v no cues	Trials (5)

Table 1 *(Continued)*

Experiment Number	*No. Ss.*	*Mean CA*	*Mean VA*	*No. items*	*No. cats.*	*No. of presentation trials*	*No. of recall trials*	*Multi or blocked trials*	*Length of presentation (seconds)*	*Length of recall (seconds)*	*No. of sessions*	*Whether naming at presentation*
1	48	12.7	5.12	6	3 or 0	6	6	Multi	25	25	3	No
2	40	23.7	4.88	6	0	6	6	Multi	30	30	2	Yes
3	40	23.7	4.88	6	3	6	6	Multi	30	30	2	Yes
4	35	24.5	7.04	–	–	–	–	–	–	–	–	–
5	72	24.8	5.89	9	3	3	1	blocked	45	45	3	Yes
6	48	26.9	7.33	9	3	2	2	blocked	45	45	3	Yes
7	80	23.7	Hi 7.95 Lo 5.75	16	4	5	5	Multi	80	80	2	Yes
8	80	23.5	7.60	16	4	3	3	blocked	60	60	1	Yes
9	32	26.6	7.82	16	4	5	5	Multi	90	60	1	No
10	64	25.7	7.86	16	4	5	5	Multi	90	60	1	No
11	80	23.7	7.96	16	4	5	5	Multi	80	80	2	Yes
12	80	23.8	5.77	16	4	5	5	Multi	80	80	2	Yes

c. Specific features of the experiments

In addition to those features which are common to all or most experiments, there are other parameters along which experiments differed from each other. These are presented in Table 1 (pp. 56-57).

References

1. BRIMER, M.A. & DUNN, L.M. (1962). *English Picture Vocabulary Tests.* Distributed by Educational Evaluation Enterprises, Bristol.
2. CLARKE, A.M., CLARKE, A.D.B., & COOPER, G.M. (1970). 'The development of a set to perceive categorical relations.' In HAYWOOD, H.C. (Ed.) *Social-cultural Aspects of Mental Retardation.* New York, Appleton-Century-Crofts.
3. GERJUOY, I.R. & ALVAREZ, J.M. (1969). 'Transfer of learning in associative clustering of retardates and normals during free recall of visual stimuli.' *American Journal of Mental Deficiency,* **73**, 791-797.
4. WINER, B.J. (1971). *'Statistical Principles in Experimental Design,'* 2nd Edition, pp. 191-201. New York, McGraw-Hill.
5. McCONKEY, R. and GREEN, J.M. (1972). The effects of presentation method on the free recall performance of adult retardates. Unpublished mss.

Postscript

An experiment has been carried out subsequently (5) designed to test the assumption stated on page 55. This was that visual simultaneous presentation of items would result in greater clustering and amount recalled than sequential presentation. There were 24 subjects, with mean CA 24, 56 (SD 7.52), mean VA 8.11 (SD 0.79), and mean BRA 8.17 (SD 1.16). The three conditions were auditory sequential, visual sequential, and visual simultaneous presentation, with total presentation time equated over conditions. The material consisted of 16 categorisable items, which were presented in a five-trial free recall procedure. The results indicated that both forms of visual presentation led to higher recall than did auditory presentation, but did not differ between themselves. There were no significant effects of condition on clustering. However, visual simultaneous presentation resulted in significantly less repetitions of items in recall than did the other two conditions. Furthermore it could still be argued that visual simultaneous presentation would facilitate clustering when the experimenter intervened in the situation; for it would provide subjects with greater opportunity of perceiving the relations between items which the experimenter was pointing out. Finally, these results suggest that the spontaneous use of a clustering strategy is independent of mode of presentation.

Chapter 7

Preliminary studies

a. Significant organisation

The preliminary studies to be described had the objective of discovering whether it would be feasible to employ the techniques of free recall with the subjects with whom we were to deal. Specifically, it was hoped to show that simultaneous visual presentation of items allows subjects ample opportunity to organise their recall; for it provides them with the chance to perceive relations between items while those items are present. Further, it was intended to demonstrate that various experimenter manipulations could have significant effects on degree of organisation. Since these studies were conceived as experiments in their own right, the results obtained may be treated with some confidence.

The major aim of Experiment 1(1) was to discover whether significant clustering (O-E) and ITR (O-E) did occur with subjects of low VA given random order presentation. Secondary aims were to investigate relations between these two measures; to investigate subjects' spontaneous naming at presentation; and to assess any differences between mongoloid and other subjects.

Specific details of Experiment 1 are presented in Table 1. Its essential features are that it presented visually and simultaneously a very few items in a multi-trial procedure to fairly young subjects (pupils at Special Schools). The material consisted of three sets, two of apparently unrelated and one of categorically related items. The latter comprised three categories with two items in each category. All subjects received the three sets of material on successive days, with the order of sets randomised. The only other feature of this experiment in which it differed from most of the other experiments was that subjects were not forced to name items in the presentation phase of the task. They were merely told to look at the pictures carefully; however, many of them spontaneously named, perhaps as a result of the preliminary naming trial.

Thus in general the situation was set up in such a way as to provide every opportunity for subjects to organise the randomly ordered items. In particular, the use of the visual modality and of simultaneous rather than successive presentation of items had this objective (2, 3). The results indicated that the objective was attained. The scores expected by chance and those actually obtained were compared for the clustering and ITR measures both for the mongoloid and for the non-mongoloid groups. For the mongoloid group, there was a highly significant difference between obtained and expected by chance clustering and ITR; for the non-mongoloid group, the difference was highly significant in the case of clustering, and just significant in the case of ITR (all t tests with correlated means). These results have been replicated in essence (4).

However, it must be stressed that the ITR scores over all subjects for the two sets of unrelated material were only just significantly correlated ($r = 0.25$). The vast variability of ITR scores over trials for each subject also suggested that it was a fragile dependent variable.

Moreover, it cannot be said that the significant clustering scores necessarily indicate that hierarchical coding processes were operating. Indeed, there were significant sequential constancies in the recall of the categorisable set of material, since obtained and expected ITR scores calculated for that set differed highly significantly. When an analysis was carried out on all the pairs of items which occurred in the same order on successive recall trials, it was found that 53% of these pairs consisted of items from the same category; only 20% would be predicted on the basis of chance. Next, analysis of all those pairs of items from the same category which occurred on successive trials were undertaken. It was found that in 63% of these pairs, the two items were in the same order on the two trials (e.g. car, train). Clearly, certain strong sequential constraints were operating.

Further, it must be stressed that although significant differences between obtained and expected measures were found, the percentage of total possible clustering was still only 37.5% and of ITR, 15%. Nevertheless, there are indications that hierarchical processes may also have been operating in the case of the categorisable material; for clustering (O-E) was highly significantly correlated with amount recalled for both mongoloid and non-mongoloid subjects; this correlation was significant in the case of non-mongoloid subjects and just significant in the case of mongoloid subjects even when the recall-independent percentage measure was employed.

In terms of the secondary aims of the experiment, no correlation between clustering scores for categorisable material and ITR scores for unrelated material was obtained. Further, ITR, unlike clustering, did not correlate with amount recalled. When subjects spontaneously named, the order of their naming bore no relation to the order of their recall; rather, it was in some directional sequence (e.g. left-to-right, top-to-bottom) corresponding to the arrangement of items on the slide.

Differences between mongoloid and non-mongoloid subjects will be discussed in Chapter 10.

b. Clustering and ITR

The primary aim of Experiments 2 and 3 (5) was to test the hypothesis that the clustering and ITR measures would function differently as dependent variables in response to the same independent variable. The independent variable was the order of labelling. That is, subjects were forced to name items at presentation in certain orders. It was reasoned that if order of labelling was different from the order in which subjects had recalled on the previous trial, then the ITR measure should be depressed. If, on the other hand, labelling was in the order of immediately previous recall, ITR should increase. Order of labelling would not be expected to affect clustering in this way, however.

Secondary aims of Experiments 2 and 3 were to discover whether there would be any changes in organisation over sessions with different material on each session; and to further investigate possible differences between mongoloid and non-mongoloid subjects.

Thus Experiments 2 and 3 do not aim to reveal how subjects spontaneously organise input; nor do they claim to discover particularly efficient ways of inducing greater organisation. Rather, the aim is the strictly limited one of producing different experimental effects upon the two measures of organisation. The details of the experiments are to be found in Table 1. The essential features are as follows. Subjects were divided into two groups, mongoloid and non-mongoloid. These two groups were further sub-divided into random-order labelling and recall-order labelling groups. The latter had to name the items at presentation in the same order as they had just previously recalled them. The experimenter pointed to each item to ensure that the required order was followed. Where subjects had recalled only e.g. 4 items, these were labelled first in recall order; then the remaining two items were labelled in random order. All subjects underwent two sessions on consecutive days. Two sets of material, consisting of apparently unrelated items, were presented, one on each session. The order of presentation of the sets was counterbalanced over sessions. Exactly the same procedure was followed a week later in Experiment 3, except that in this case the material was categorisable. The same subjects, randomly re-allocated to groups, were employed.

Results were as follows. Labelling in recall order led to greater ITR (O-E) than labelling in random order; the difference was highly significant. In the case of categorisable material, the converse was found: labelling in recall order led to just significantly less clustering (O-E) than labelling in random order. However, a significant three-way interaction effect revealed that this was only true for non-mongoloid subjects on day 1 and for mongoloid subjects on day 2.

Thus the basic hypothesis that manipulation of the order of labelling would have different effects on the two measures of organisation was in part confirmed. The nature of the manipulation suggested that the ITR measure reflects a sequential recall strategy in which each item cues the next. However, once again there were no effects of conditions on amount recalled, so there is no evidence that the subjects who clustered were employing an hierarchical strategy. Once again, the percentage of total possible clustering was well below 50%.

The results of Experiments 1, 2 and 3 suggested that clustering was a viable dependent variable with subjects of the ability level employed in these experiments. However, no satisfactory evidence of an hierarchical coding of relations which might result in information reduction and consequent greater recall had been obtained. It was therefore decided to provide category codings for the subjects. By this means it might be determined whether subnormal subjects are capable of employing codings to aid recall.

The subsequent use of unrelated items and the ITR measures was rejected, since subjective organisation was not reliable. Further, it rarely reached a level of above 15% of maximum possible, and appeared to offer less opportunity of investigating hierarchical processes which reduce information load.

Before category cues were employed, however, it seemed necessary to ensure that subjects were capable of utilising the category relations present in categorisable material; and to discover whether they could on request supply category codings of their own which resembled or were the same as those provided by the experimenter.

c. *Sorting and labelling*

One task which might be expected to demonstrate whether subjects could identify which items belong together is that of sorting. For it permits subjects to scan an array in order to perceive relations; it also allows them (at least in the present experiment) to see the items they have already sorted, and, if necessary, modify their sorts.

Research on category sorting with the subnormal has stressed the apparent inability of these subjects to supply verbal labels to categories, the items of which they have already successfully sorted (6,7). The general conclusion has been that Luria's theory of a verbal mediation deficiency is supported by these findings; that is, it is inferred that subnormal individuals are unlikely to be capable of using verbal mediators to regulate their behaviour. If this conclusion is justified, then the provision by the experimenter of category cues in the free recall task should not be beneficial. For subnormal subjects would be incapable of using the cues to store and retrieve items by. It is possible, however, that the relationship between sorting and labelling categories is more complex. Subjects may be capable of sorting, and also of labelling; however the tasks may require different skills respectively. The sorter has to see the relationship between all the items in a category, whereas the labeller may have to supply a superordinate to one item only. For the labeller may name a category as a result of applying a superordinate to one or two of the items; he does not need to ensure that the label is appropriate to all the items if he is to be credited with a correct response. Thus the successful labeller and the successful sorter are not necessarily synonymous; in order to employ successfully his labelling for use in any sorting or recall task, the subject has to subsume *all* the category items under the category label.

The results of Experiment 4 (8) support this latter point of view. Subjects were given three successive sorting tasks, with each task requiring them to sort 16 pictorially presented items into 4 categories. Instructions were to put together the things that belong together. After each sorting trial, subjects were asked why the things they had put together belonged together. At least a day later, subjects were shown slides, each of which presented the four items from each of the categories; the categories were the experimenter-defined ones rather than any idiosyncratic groupings which subjects may have sorted. They were then asked 'Why do all these things belong together?'. If this brought no response, the experimenter further asked 'What do we do with them all?' or 'What are they all for?' There was thus a sorting task, a label sort task, and a labelling task. Only 9 out of the 35 subjects completely failed to sort. Sorting scores could range from 0 to 102, the latter being the maximum possible total score for the three sortings.

Points were allocated on the basis of degree of completeness of the category. In the case of labelling, scores ranged from 0 to 12. Success at sorting was highly significantly correlated with success at the label sort task (r = .97). However, it was much less highly correlated with the labelling task (r = .59). In other words, those subjects who were able to sort were invariably capable of applying a verbal label to their sorting; however, when subjects were presented with the items already sorted into their categories, one category at a time, performance on sorting did not necessarily predict success at labelling. Indeed, even the 9 subjects who completely failed to sort succeeded in labelling a mean of 8.2 categories. Moreover, it was found that the categories which subjects found easiest to sort were not necessarily the ones they found easiest to label. The rank order correlation between sorting and label sort was .59, and that between sorting and labelling .53; the label sort and the labelling tasks correlated .85, however.

Thus while subjects in general could sort categories and also label them, the relation between sorting and labelling was shown to be a complex one. The implications for the free recall task using categorisable material appear to be as follows. Since subjects were capable of labelling without being able to sort, the possibility remains that they were applying category labels to one or more items from the category only, rather than to the category as a whole. Therefore the experimenter supplying category labels in the free recall task in order to provide superordinate codings should associate them with each and every item which they subsume. Secondly, if the subject is given the opportunity to sort the items himself, he is highly likely to be able to supply his own superordinate codings. Both these implications are carried through in the subsequent series of experiments. In particular, a mode of cueing at presentation was usually employed which presented the appropriate cue after the subject had named each item.

d. Cues – their nature and locus

Experiments 5 and 6 endeavoured to evidence secondary processes by providing superordinate cues after each item. Experiment 5 provided different types of cue at presentation, while Experiment 6 provided verbal cues at presentation, at recall, and at both presentation and recall. In both experiments, 9 items were employed for the task, 3 categories with 3 items per category; there were three sessions on successive days, with different material for each session.

Dealing first with Experiment 5, the procedure followed at each session was that of multi-trial presentation followed by a single recall trial. The purpose of the three immediately successive presentation trials was to emphasise the connexion between cues and items. There were three main factors, aetiology (mongoloid versus non-mongoloid), conditions, and days (the latter being a repeated measures factor). The conditions were no cues, verbal cues, miming cues, and both miming and verbal cues. Miming cues were employed since it seemed important to discover whether non-verbal superordinates were especially beneficial for a population of low verbal ability. In all cases the subject was presented with the 9 items pictorially and required to name each in a random order, with the experimenter pointing to the one to be named. In the case of the verbal cues condition, after the subject named each item, the experimenter would say "for eating", "for wearing", or whatever the appropriate cue to that item was. In the case of miming cues, the experimenter acted out the action associated with that category of items, employing the same mime for all items within a category.

Results in terms of amount recalled were disappointing. There was no overall conditions effect, so superordinate cues provided by the experimenter did not improve recall. This cannot be attributed to a ceiling effect, since overall mean recall was only 6.06 out of a possible 9 items. There was, however, a significant effect of aetiology, with mongoloid subjects recalling less than non-mongoloid subjects. There was also a just significant overall days effect, with recall on day 2 significantly worse than that on days 1 and 3, which did not differ from each other.

Results in terms of clustering (O-E), on the other hand, did show a just significant conditions effect. This was only true of non-mongoloid subjects, however. This conditions effect, when further analysed, indicated that verbal cues alone and miming cues alone were both just significantly more effective than no cues and both verbal and miming cues together. However, verbal cues did not differ from miming cues, nor did no cues from both verbal and miming cues together. Thus the single cues increased clustering over a no cues condition in the case of non-mongoloid subjects but the double cues did not. Further conditions were employed in order to discover why the double cues were not effective. When two verbal cues were employed, clustering performance was midway between that of the single verbal cue and the verbal plus miming cue conditions. Thus neither an explanation in terms of overall information load nor one in terms specifically of bi-modality was indicated.

Additionally, a just significant days effect on clustering was obtained. Further analysis showed that day 3 was just significantly superior to days 1 and 2, which did not themselves differ.

Thus while effects of cues on clustering were found, no such effects were found on amount recalled. Furthermore, no significant correlations between clustering (%) and amount recalled were obtained. It therefore seemed appropriate to discover whether more effective use of codings might be obtained if verbal cues were provided at different phases of the procedure. Cues were provided at presentation, at recall, and at both presentation and recall. It was hypothesised that the latter condition would result in increased recall, since the cues provided at presentation were reinstated at recall and made available for retrieval purposes.

In Experiment 6, two successive presentation trials were followed by two successive recall trials. This procedure most effectively permits the effects of presentation and recall cues to be distinguished. Subjects were all non-mongoloid. The main factors were conditions, days, and recall trials, with the latter two factors repeated measures. Verbal presentation cues were given in the same way as in Experiment 5; in addition, recall cues were supplied by the experimenter in the same manner as Gerjuoy and Spitz's (9) requested clustered condition (see p. 45). The subject was asked, for example, 'What animals were there?'. When he was silent for a few seconds another cue was presented; when he uttered an item from another category, the appropriate category cue would be provided. The condition in which both presentation and recall cues were given was simply a combination of the two single cue conditions.

Once again, no conditions effect on amount recalled was obtained. However, there was a significant conditions effect on clustering (O-E). Presentation cues did not differ significantly from no cues; nor did recall cues from both presentation and recall cues together. However, both the latter conditions resulted in just significantly more clustering than both the former conditions. The absence of an effect of presentation cues in Experiment 6 may be explained in terms of the considerable clustering evidenced in the no cue condition. This was greater than the clustering in the miming cues and the verbal cues conditions in Experiment 5, and could be a function of the higher mean VA of the subjects employed in Experiment 6 (7.33 as opposed to 5.89). The increased clustering arising out of the use of recall cues is hardly surprising, as the experimenter is actively requesting recall in clustered order. The fact that recall cues alone are as effective in inducing clustering as the condition where cues are given both at presentation and at recall probably supports this explanation.

In addition, there was a just significant effect on clustering of days, and a highly significant effect of trials. In the case of days, day 1 was just significantly inferior to day 2, and was significantly inferior also to day 3. In the case of trials, trial 1 was inferior to trial 2. The trials effect is interesting since it indicates that the first recall trial may have acted as a learning trial (10). This may have been due to subjects becoming better at retrieving items by categories (11), or to their perceiving more relations between items as a result of recall (12). It cannot be attributed to a recency effect operating on the first trial only; for analysis showed that the last item presented was no more likely to occur first in recall than any other item.

Once again, however, neither effects on amount recalled nor positive correlations of clustering (%) with amount recalled had been obtained. Therefore firm evidence of secondary process was not available. There seemed one likely explanation: ceiling effects were operating. Many subjects in the cued conditions achieved total correct recall.

In sum, preliminary studies showed that simultaneous visual presentation was a viable means of obtaining clustering in recall. The effects of cues on clustering suggested that experimenter intervention of this nature could be effective. And improvement in clustering over days suggested the possibility that subjects could learn to organise. Results had also suggested experimental manipulations by which secondary processes might be evidenced, e.g. active sorting of items by subjects. They also suggested the dangers of ceiling effects. However, it must be stressed that these preliminary studies failed to provide any firm evidence of secondary processes.

References

1. HERRIOT, P. & COX, A.M. (1971). 'Subjective organisation and clustering in the free recall of intellectually subnormal children.' *American Journal of Mental Deficiency,* **75**, 702-711.
2. GERJUOY, I.R., WINTERS, J.J., PULLEN, M.M., & SPITZ, H.H. (1969). 'Subjective organisation by retardates and normals during free recall of visual stimuli.' *American Journal of Mental Deficiency,* **73**, 791-797.
3. GERJUOY, I.R. & WINTERS, J.J. (1970). 'Subjective

organisation by EMR adolescents in free recall: bimodal presentation.' *American Journal of Mental Deficiency*, **74**, 509-516.

4. McCOY, M. Unpublished B.A. thesis, Queens University, Belfast.
5. HERRIOT, P. (1972). 'The effect of order of labelling on the subjective organisation and clustering of severely retarded adults.' *American Journal of Mental Deficiency*, 76, 632-638.
6 BLOUNT, W.R. (1968). 'Concept usage research with the mentally retarded.' *Psychological Bulletin*, **69**, 281-294.
7. STEPHENS, W.E. (1966). 'Category usage by normal and mentally retarded boys.' *Child Development*, **37**, 355-361.
8. McCONKEY, R. and HERRIOT, P. 'The relationship between category labelling and sorting with adult retardates.' *American Journal of Mental Deficiency*, (in press)
9. GERJUOY, I.R. & SPITZ, H.H. (1966). 'Associative clustering in free recall: intellectual and developmental variables.' *American Journal of Mental Deficiency*, **70**, 918-927.
10. LACHMAN, R. & LAUGHERY, K.R. (1968). 'Is a test trial a training trial in free recall learning?' *Journal of Experimental Psychology*, **76**, 40-50.
11. DONALDSON, W. (1971). 'Output effects in multi-trial free recall.' *Journal of Verbal Learning and Verbal Behavior*, **10**, 577-582.
12. LEWIS, M.Q. (1971). 'Short-term memory items in repeated free recall.' *Journal of Verbal Learning and Verbal Behavior*, **10**, 190-193.

Chapter 8

Category cues

a. Cues at presentation and recall

Chapters 8 and 9 describe more experiments which employed various forms of experimenter intervention. Such intervention is appropriate since uncued performance offers little indication that these subjects can organise spontaneously in such a way as to increase amount recalled. While a statistically significant degree of clustering may occur, it does not appear to affect amount recalled. Furthermore this seems to be a consistent finding. Performance on the no cues control conditions by subjects of higher vocabulary age (VA) in Experiment 7 and in Experiment 9, for instance, are remarkably similar. Although there were differences in these experiments (e.g. presentation by means of cards in Experiment 9 as opposed to the projected presentation of Experiment 7), nevertheless mean clustering (O-E) was 1.04 and 1.19 respectively, and mean recall 10.14 and 9.80. Even the subjects of considerably lower VA also employed in experiment 7 did not differ markedly in their non-cued performance; their mean clustering score was 1.00 and their mean recall score 9.41. In all cases the percentage of maximum possible clustering obtained was low (never above 20%). This failure to organise spontaneously to any appreciable extent does not, however, justify a deficiency inference. Rather, it suggests the importance of exploring different modes of intervention in an effort significantly to induce performance above this level.

Experiment 7(1) was designed to test further the hypothesis that category cues provided by the experimenter will increase amount recalled. The most favourable cueing procedure appeared to be that of both presentation and recall cues, with presentation cues being provided after each item. The reasons for this decision have already been discussed on p. 64. The justification for carrying out another experiment employing the same procedure as two of the conditions of Experiment 6 was that this previous experiment's failure to find a significant effect on recall was presumed to be due to a ceiling effect. In Experiment 7, the number of items to be recalled was therefore increased from 9 to 16.

Another factor varied in Experiment 7 was vocabulary age (VA). Subjects of higher and lower verbal ability were treated as separate groups. An indication that this might be an important variable was the performance of the control groups in Experiments 5 and 6, where lower and higher VA subjects respectively were employed (see p. 66). Differences found in Experiment 7 between subjects of differing VA will be discussed in more detail in Chapter 10. Subjects' performance on a second session in Experiment 7, in which all subjects received the same uncued condition, will also be discussed in Chapter 10.

In Experiment 7, cued and uncued conditions were employed for subjects of higher and of lower VA. The procedure was that of multi-trial free recall; that is, each of five presentation trials was immediately followed by a recall trial. The cueing procedure was identical to that employed in Experiment 6 (see p. 66).

Figure 1 indicates results in terms of amount recalled. Subjects of higher VA were highly significantly superior in amount recalled to subjects of lower VA. Amount recalled increased highly significantly over trials. And there was a just significant superiority of cued over non-cued subjects. This overall superiority was, however, attributable entirely to the fact that cues gave rise to a highly significant increase in amount recalled for the higher VA group, but made no difference to lower VA subjects; this interaction effect of cueing with VA was statistically significant. Moreover, subjects of higher VA improved more over trials than subjects of lower VA; again, this interaction was statistically significant. Differences associated with VA are discussed in Chapter 10.

The results in terms of clustering showed a similar pattern. On all measures of clustering, the same highly significant main effects were found as for amount recalled. Furthermore, the same interaction of VA with cues (that subjects of higher VA clustered more as a result of cues than subjects of lower VA) was also found. Cues did result in an increase in clustering in subjects of low VA, however.

Thus the hypothesis that superordinate cues provided at both presentation and recall would increase not just clustering but also amount recalled had been confirmed. Since the result was obtained with bi-modally presented material, the suggestion of Gerjuoy and Winters (2) that amount recalled and clustering will only be related in the case of auditory presentation was contradicted. It is therefore a very significant finding.

b. The function of cues

Experiment 8 (3) was designed, firstly, to discover in what way the cueing procedure employed in Experiment 7 had been effective in

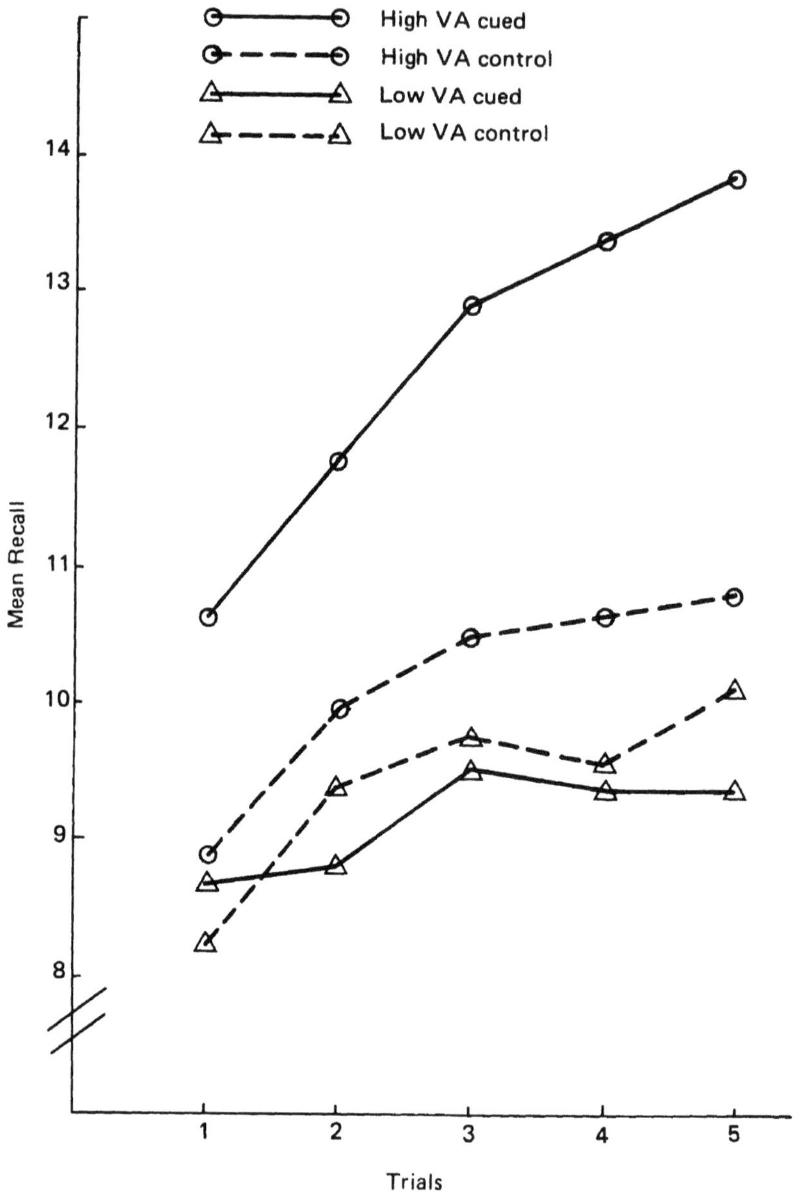

Figure 1 *Mean Recall scores on five consecutive trials of subjects in Experiment 7 (20 Ss per group) Day 1.*

improving amount recalled. The respective functions of cues at presentation and recall have already been discussed (see pp. 15,24). To recapitulate, it is suggested that if cues at both presentation and recall are superior to cues at presentation only, this implies that subjects are benefited by having the cues made available to them for retrieval purposes (instead of having to retain them or otherwise reconstruct them themselves). If cues at both presentation and recall are superior to cues at recall only, this implies that subjects benefit from being supplied with codings at presentation which they may not have been able to supply adequately for themselves.

A second objective of Experiment 8 was to investigate further the relation of clustering to amount recalled. Experiment 7 had shown, for subjects of high VA, a high degree of similarity in the effects of independent variables on clustering and recall. However, there appear to be theoretical grounds for assuming that there are differences. Specifically, it might be supposed that cues provided at recall only will increase clustering but will not increase amount recalled. Such cues provided subjects with a coding and instructions to use it to generate the items it subsumes. This is simply an invitation to exercise semantic and categorical skills, and check that the items thus generated were among those presented. Clearly, such a procedure almost guarantees increased clustering. However, it need not result in increased recall. For if the analysis of the previous paragraph is correct, superordinate codings are required at presentation and must be reinstated at recall. Thus different effects of presentation and recall cues are predicted for clustering and amount recalled.

In order to achieve these two objectives, two sets of material were prepared. They both consisted of 16 items which were all manufactured articles; their colour was therefore relatively arbitrary. In the first, compatible set, the items from the same category were all of the same colour; in the second, incompatible set, they were all of different colours. There were five cueing conditions: 1, no cues; 2, presentation cues; 3, recall cues; 4, presentation and recall cues when both were category labels; 5, presentation and recall cues when presentation cues were names of colours, and recall cues were category labels. Thus, for example, in the last condition the experimenter would say at presentation 'Now let's look at the yellow things; there's a ....' (experimenter points to all yellow things, which subject had to name). Clearly, this condition will be different in the case of the two sets of material. When items from the same category are of the same colour, each colour name presentation cue will be referring to the same items as its appropriate category label recall cue. But in the set where colour and function are not identical, category as well as cue will be different at presentation and recall. The purpose of these conditions was to create a situation in which the limits of the effects of recall cues on clustering might be explored.

Other basic features of Experiment 8 were, firstly, that three successive presentation trials were followed by three recall trials. This was to distinguish as far as possible the effects of presentation cues from those of recall cues. For the usual multi-trial procedure means that cues which had just been provided at recall might be available for the next presentation trial. Secondly, the cueing procedure at presentation involved the experimenter providing the category name, then pointing to the four appropriate items and requiring the subject to name them. In other words, presentation was blocked, in the sense that items from the same category were named successively by the subjects. Thus both item relations and superordinates were being assisted by the experimenter. Recall cues were provided in the same way as in Experiments 6 and 7.

Results on amount recalled were as follows (see Table 2). The only, just significant, effect on amount recalled was that of conditions. Further analysis showed that the condition in which category label cues were provided at both presentation and recall was superior to all other conditions. It was highly significantly superior to the no cues condition, whereas no other condition was superior to this control condition. Thus the only form of assistance which increased amount recalled over the control condition was that in which both presentation and recall cues were category labels. Its superiority over the presentation cues condition indicates the importance of retaining codings and seeing their use for retrieval; its superiority over recall cues shows the importance of applying codings at presentation; and its superiority over the condition in which presentation and recall cues differ demonstrates the importance of the identity of presentation and recall codings and categories throughout the recall task.

The second aim of Experiment 8 was to investigate further the relation between clustering and amount recalled. Effects on clustering were quite different from those for amount recalled (see Table 2). There was a highly significant conditions effect, but when this was further analysed, it became evident that any form of cueing resulted in increased clustering over the no cues condition. For all other conditions resulted in significantly more clustering than the no cues condition on all measures of clustering employed.

Although all forms of cueing increased clustering, the only major

Table 2 *Recall and clustering scores (means and SDs) for all conditions for Experiment 8, pooled over trials.*

Set	*Compatible*									
Conditions	*N*		*P*		*R*		*CPR*		*PR*	
Measure	*Mean*	*SD*	*Mean*	*SD*	*Mean*	*SD*	*Mean*	*SD*	*Mean*	*SD*
Recall	9.71	2.26	10.1	2.92	10.3	1.93	11.0	2.84	11.9	3.67
O - E	0.39	1.05	2.71	2.98	4.03	1.66	4.90	2.33	5.68	2.75
%	8.79	32.3	50.7	42.5	86.7	19.0	87.9	30.2	96.4	14.3
Z Score	–0.91	1.30	0.32	2.86	2.45	1.71	2.66	3.77	3.89	1.89
Set	*Incompatible*									
Conditions	*N*		*P*		*R*		*CPR*		*PR*	
Measure	*Mean*	*SD*	*Mean*	*SD*	*Mean*	*SD*	*Mean*	*SD*	*Mean*	*SD*
Recall	9.46	2.25	10.5	3.66	8.92	3.12	9.75	2.21	13.5	2.77
O - E	0.73	1.20	3.17	2.98	3.11	1.98	3.47	2.05	6.59	2.40
%	20.5	36.1	50.5	70.5	82.1	29.0	81.0	28.1	92.2	13.6
Z Score	0.11	1.53	0.99	2.69	2.11	1.82	2.47	1.82	4.23	2.01

Key *N* = no cues, *P* = presentation cues, *R* = recall cues, *CPR* = presentation cues colour names, recall cues category labels, *PR* = both presentation and recall cues category labels.

difference in effectiveness *between* forms of cueing was the significant inferiority of presentation cues alone to the condition in which presentation and recall cues were category labels. As one might expect, any condition in which subjects were requested to recall in categorised order was highly effective in inducing clustering.

The absence of any effect of sets on either recall or clustering suggests that at least in situations in which subjects name the items, incidental perceptual features such as colour are of no importance.

To summarise, Experiment 8 repeated the finding of Experiment 7 that hierarchical coding processes are available to adult subnormals of higher VA when presented bi-modally. And it indicated that amount recalled and clustering vary in different ways in response to several different forms of cueing.

References

1. GREEN, J.M. (1973). 'The use of category cues in free recall by retarded adults of two vocabulary age levels'. *American Journal of Mental Deficiency*, (in press).
2. GERJUOY, I.R. & WINTERS, J.J. (1970). 'Subjective organisation by EMR adolescents in free recall: bi-modal presentation.' *American Journal of Mental Deficiency*, 74, 509-516.
3. HERRIOT, P. (1972). 'The effect of category cues on the free recall of retarded adults.' *Psychonomic Science*, 28, 341-342.

Chapter 9

Other experimental interventions

a. Grouping and cues

The results of Experiments 7 and 8 pointed to two further lines of research. The first concerned assistance at presentation. Since recall cues alone were not effective in increasing amount recalled, a closer investigation of the nature of subjects' coding processes at presentation seemed appropriate. For efficient coding at presentation is a necessary condition for the reduction of information load. Experiments 9 and 10 (1) had this objective. Experiment 9 was designed to investigate the relative effects of cueing and grouping (see p. 48).

Previous research had shown that items blocked by category were recalled better than randomly presented items when presentation was auditory (2). However, grouping had been found (3) to increase clustering but not recall of bimodally presented items. It might be supposed that grouping permitted subjects to perceive inter-item associations more readily. It might also have been expected to assist subjects to supply a superordinate coding, since all the category items were placed in juxtaposition and were presented simultaneously. However, the absence of any effects on amount recalled in the Gerjuoy and Winters experiment suggests that subjects did not supply their own superordinates. It was therefore hypothesised that the provision of cues would meet this deficiency and that grouped presentation and category cues would thus provide assistance for both inter-item associations and superordinate codings.

Since the purpose of the experiment was to investigate the effects of experimenter intervention on coding at storage, presentation cues only were provided. This method permits a far more meaningful analysis of organisation than does any form of cueing which requires subjects to recall in categorical order. Moreover, an additional criterion for subject selection was included in Experiments 9 and 10. Simple sorting and labelling tasks were employed for this purpose; all subjects had to succeed in sorting 6 items into two categories and in labelling ten common categories to a 75% correct criterion. Items, too, were chosen on the basis that they were easy to recognise and sort (see Experiment 4). The purpose of these criteria was to ensure that subjects were as familiar as possible with the categories and their labels employed in the experiment. Other features which distinguish Experiments 9 and 10 from other experiments are, firstly, that material was not projected. Rather, each item was drawn on a white card. This was to meet the need for manipulation by subjects in Experiment 10. Finally, subjects were not required to name items at presentation.

There were thus four groups of subjects, 1, no cues and random order presentation. 2, no cues and grouped presentation. 3, cues and random presentation. 4, cues and grouped presentation. The cards were presented on a board. For grouped presentation, the four items from any one category were placed adjacently in the same corner of the board. For random presentation, on the other hand, all 16 items were placed around the middle of the board. They were so arranged that no two items from the same category were immediately adjacent.

The subjects in the cued conditions were told that if they looked carefully, they would see that some of the things belonged together. There were things for eating, things for driving, some animals, and things for wearing. They were to look at all the things there were for eating (20 seconds' pause), things for driving (20 seconds' pause), things for wearing (20 seconds' pause) ...etc. Position of items and of categories and order of cues were randomly varied over trials.

There were thus three factors: presence versus absence of cues, grouped versus random presentation, and trials as a repeated measure. When amount recalled was analysed (see Figure 2) the only significant main effect was that of trials; this was highly significant. There was also a just significant grouping by trials interaction, with grouping leading to a greater increase in recall over trials than random order presentation. Finally, there was a just significant grouping by cues by trials interaction; examination of Figure 2 suggests that this was the result of a ceiling effect operating on the cues plus grouping condition. When a multiple regression analysis was carried out, holding subject variables constant, just significant effects of grouping were found on four of the five trials; that is, subjects in the grouped conditions recalled more. When a similar analysis for cueing was carried out, no effects on amount recalled were found.

When effects on measures of clustering were analysed (see Table 3), highly significant grouping effects and significant or highly significant cueing effects were found; both grouping and cues increased organisation. A highly significant trials effect was found only for the recall-dependent

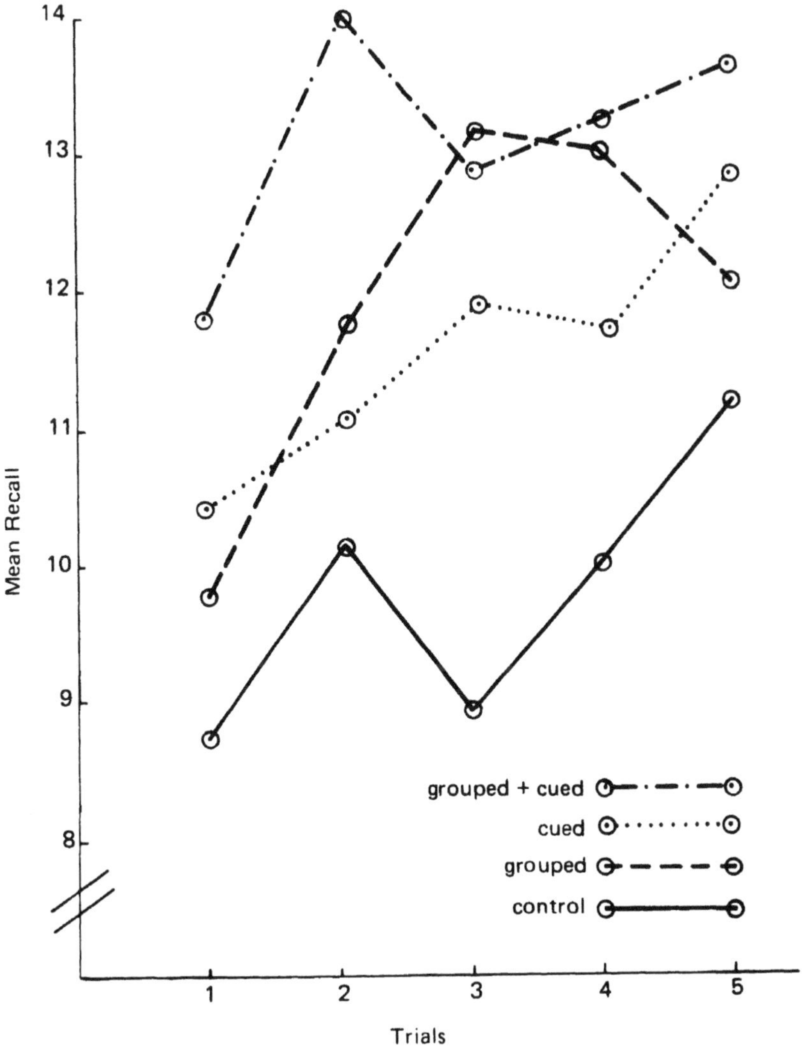

Figure 2 *Mean recall scores on five consecutive trials of subjects in Experiment 9 (8 Ss per group).*

Table 3 *Means and standard deviations of clustering scores, pooled over trials, of subjects in Experiment 9, using three different measures of clustering (8 Ss per group)*

	Condition	*Control*	*Cued*	*Grouped*	*Cued & Grouped*
Measure	O-E	1.04	4.40	5.20	6.73
		(1.59)	(3.39)	(2.45)	(2.56)
	%	15.3	62.2	84.2	97.5
		(54.7)	(42.9)	(26.0)	(7.90)
	Z	0.33	2.98	3.82	4.63
		(1.57)	(2.25)	(1.53)	(2.38)

O-E measure. Again, no significant interaction effects were found. However, inspection of Table 3 reveals that cueing was more beneficial during random presentation than during grouped presentation ($p < .06$). It is also noteworthy that grouping produced a nearly maximal degree of clustering.

The finding that presentation cues did not result in increased recall repeats the findings of Experiments 5 and 8. The provision of superordinates alone is insufficient to improve recall. However, the main effect of grouping on recall, together with the absence of any interaction with cues, suggests that grouping may result in assistance to both superordinates and inter-item associations.* This interpretation is supported by the finding that cues plus grouping resulted in no greater recall than grouping alone; and secondly, by the nearly significant interaction of cues with grouping on clustering. This interaction implies that cueing had little effect when presentation was grouped. Perhaps the effect of grouping is analogous to that of presentation plus recall cues, insofar as both superordinates and inter-item associations are stressed.

Whatever the reason for the facilitatory effect of grouping, its possibilities merited further investigation. In particular, it seemed important to discover whether subjects could form their own groupings, instead of having to rely upon passive reception of a structure imposed by the experimenter. If this were found to be so, it could be concluded that specific assistance by the experimenter is not necessary for the use of secondary processes.

* See Postscript on page 86.

b. Sorting and instructions

One variable manipulated in Experiment 10 was therefore the presence or absence of opportunity to actively sort the items into groupings on the board. The other was the degree of constraint of instructions as to how subjects could sort. It was hypothesised that specific cues or instructions to organise would be of more benefit to subjects in the passive condition than to those in the active condition. This was based on the assumption that active subjects would be able to group items, and in so doing would provide themselves with codings or other aids to organisation. Four types of instruction were therefore given; first category cues; second, information that the material was categorisable; third, instructions to group in fours; and, finally, instructions to re-organise the randomly presented material in whatever way subjects wished.

There were thus three factors; active versus passive sorting, instructions, and trials (the latter a repeated measure). Of the 8 groups thus formed, two of the passive conditions had already been carried out in Experiment 9, and these results were therefore used in Experiment 10. The conditions in question were the passive cued and the passive 'generally rearrange' conditions. For all groups, material was presented in random order in the middle of a board; the active groups were then encouraged to put the items in the corners of the board, while the passive sorting groups were merely told to think of the items. Thus, for example, the groups who received the instruction that the material was categorisable were told 'Put the ones you think belong together into the same corner' (active sorting group) or 'Think of all the things that you think belong together' (passive sorting group).

Once again, there were no significant effects on amount recalled. However, there were significant effects of all three factors on all measures of clustering. Considering the percentage measure specifically as typical (see Figure 3), the sorting factor was just significant, with the active group exceeding the passive group. Instructions were highly significant; further analysis showed that the provision of category cues at presentation led to significantly more clustering than all other modes of instruction; and that information that the material was categorisable resulted in just significantly more clustering than instructions to re-organise in whatever way subjects wished. There was also a highly significant improvement over trials. Finally, there was one just significant interaction effect; instructions interacted with trials, indicating

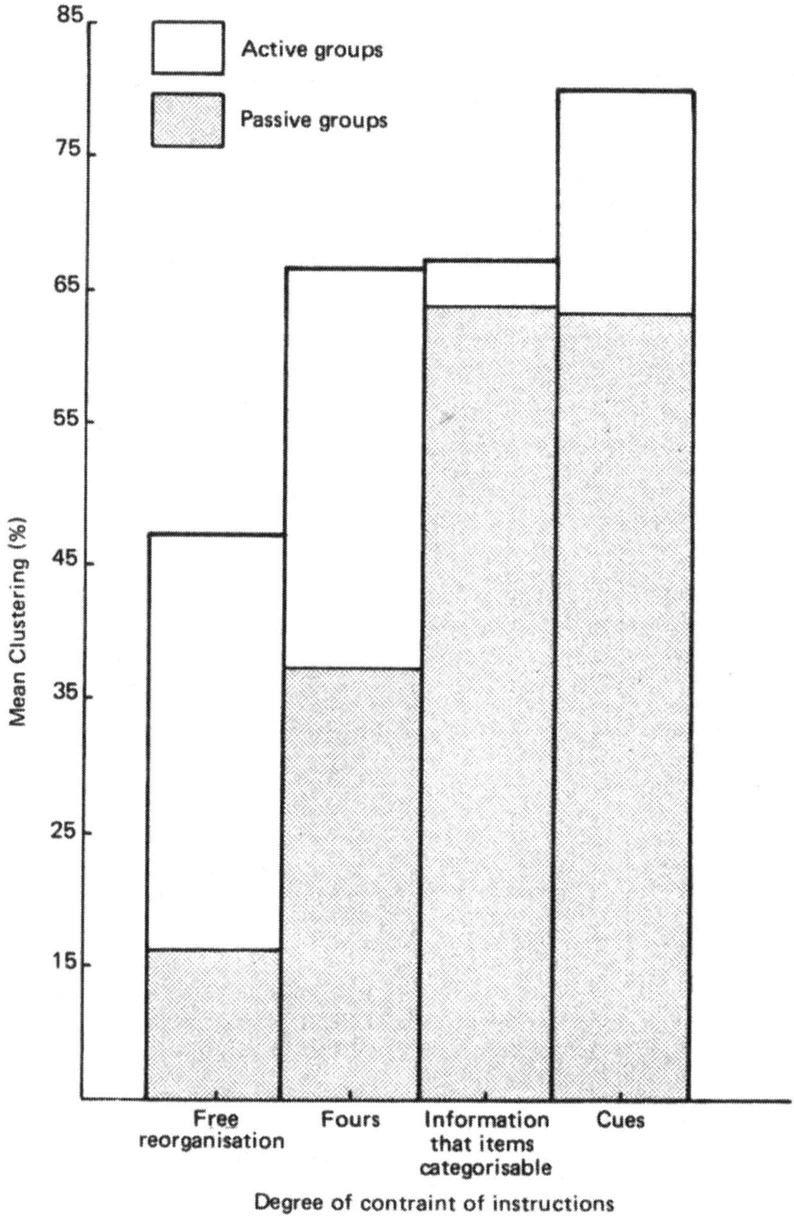

Figure 3 *Mean clustering (%) scores pooled over trials of subjects in Experiment 10 (8 Ss per group).*

that improvement over trials was greater when information was provided that the material was categorisable.

Thus there were significant sorting and instructions effects, but the predicted interaction did not occur. The effects of instructions and of active sorting were additive, suggesting that the opportunity to sort into groups and the provision of instructions aid organisation in different ways. Indeed, sorting increases organisation over and above any form of instruction.

The absence of effects on amount recalled appeared due to the high intra-group variance obtained. This variance was attributable to instructions. In an attempt to reduce it, further analysis of the results was carried out. The 8 subjects from all the active sorting conditions were selected who had a mean sorting score over trials of greater than 90% of the maximum possible organisation. These subjects were termed groupers. They were balanced with the 8 subjects who scored less than 30% correctly sorted (non-groupers). These two groups were compared with two passive groups of Experiment 9, the passive grouped and passive random conditions. These were taken to be the comparable passive groups to the groupers and non-groupers respectively. Thus the three factors in the analysis were grouping versus non-grouping, active versus passive, and trials. Analysis showed that the grouped conditions recalled just significantly more than the non-grouped conditions, but that there was no effect due to the active versus passive factor. Thus when items were grouped, either by the subject or the experimenter, recall was greater than when items were randomly arranged.

It therefore appears to be the case that grouping per se results in increased recall, rather than the opportunity to actively sort into groups. Nevertheless, the finding of Experiment 10 that subjects *can* sort into groups and consequently improve recall is of considerable importance. It indicates that they are not dependent upon highly specific forms of experimenter assistance such as cueing, blocking, or grouping, to organise. The next section confirms this emphasis, since it indicates the potential of general instructions to cluster to improve both organisation (as in Experiment 10) *and* amount recalled.

c. General instructions to organise

The finding of Experiment 10 that specific forms of assistance are not necessary for increased organisation and recall, suggests further investigation of general instructions to organise by categories. It was, for example, noted in Experiment 10 that the active group who received cues were no better at sorting into categories than the active group who received general instructions. However, general instructions had not resulted in increased recall in Experiment 10. The hypothesis would be, then, that general instructions would be as efficient as cues in improving clustering and amount recalled.

Subjects for Experiment 11 (4) were all of the same higher VA as the subjects in Experiments 8, 9, and 10. Presentation was projected, and there were five presentation and recall trials in a multi-trial procedure. The three factors were presence versus absence of cues, presence versus absence of general instructions, and trials (the latter a repeated measure). The cues only and control conditions were identical to those in Experiment 7, and therefore the results of the high VA subjects in that experiment were employed here. The four conditions were thus no cues or instructions, cues only, instructions only, and cues plus instructions.*

The precise nature of the instructions was as follows. After initial naming of items and before the first presentation trial, the experimenter said 'I'm going to show you those pictures again. If you have a good look at them, you'll see that some of the things belong together. If you think of the ones that go together, it might help you remember them better'. Before each subsequent presentation trial, she said 'Let's have another look at the pictures, looking specially at the ones which belong together'. Before each recall trial, she said 'Now tell me the things that belonged together'. If subjects completed their naming of the items at presentation before the presentation period of 80 seconds was complete, the experimenter said 'Just keep looking at the things that belong together'. Similar instructions without the last three words were given to subjects in non-instructed conditions.

In terms of amount recalled, results indicated (see Figure 4) that the presence of cues resulted in greater recall; that the same was true of instructions; and that subjects' recall improved over trials. All these results were highly significant. There were, however, no interaction effects.

The same highly significant results were obtained for clustering. In addition, several (but not all) of the measures showed a highly significant cues x trials interaction. This was due to the fact that cued subjects improved over trials more than uncued subjects.

Thus the suggestion provided by Experiment 10 that information that items belonged together could lead to increased organisation was amply confirmed. Instructions alone were capable of increasing amount

* This experiment was subsequently repeated with subjects of low VA. See Postscript A, page 96.

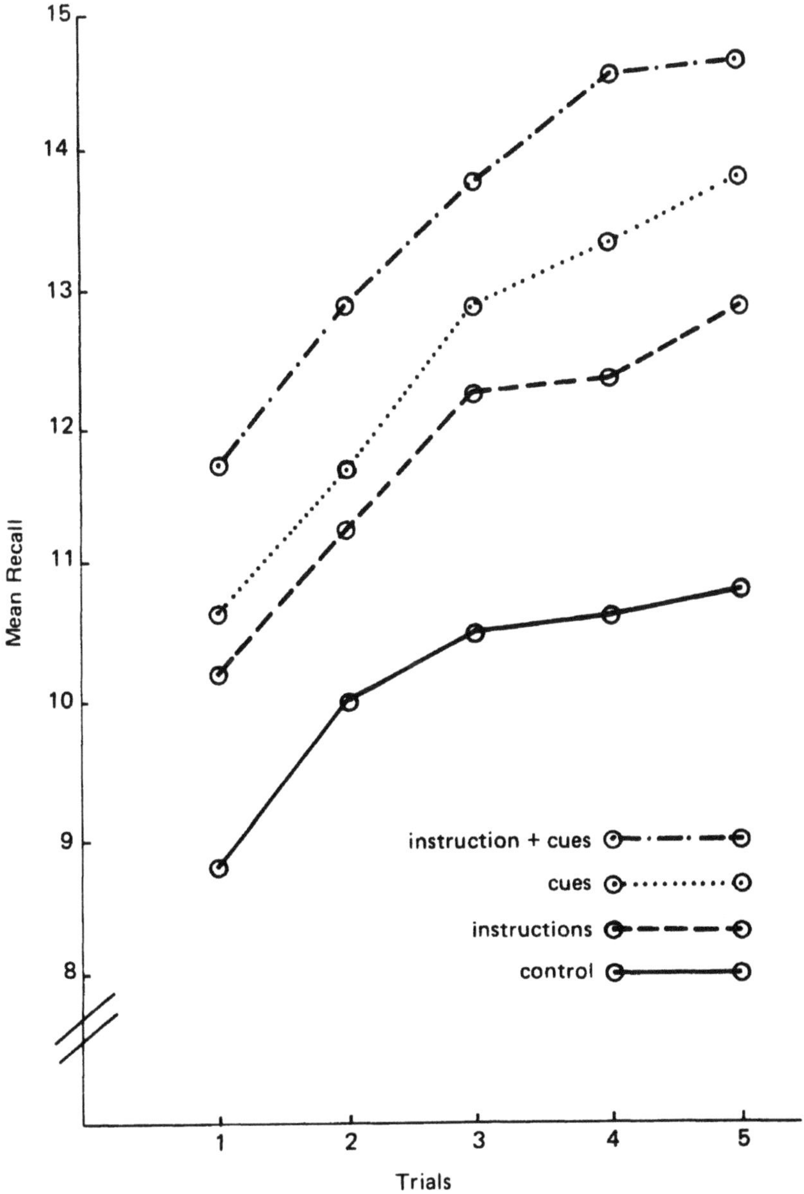

Figure 4 *Mean recall scores on five consecutive trials of subjects in Experiment 11 (20 Ss per group), Day 1.*

recalled and clustering. This implies that non-instructed subjects had the tools available, perhaps in the form of superordinate codings and inter-item relations. However, they did not see that the experimental situation was an appropriate task for their use. Since they had probably never before been faced with such a task, this is hardly surprising. The point must be reiterated as forcefully as possible that failure to apply a strategy to a task does not imply that the strategy is not available at all. This facilitatory effect of instructions clearly shows that subjects do have organisational strategies available for use. Their difficulty may often lie in not seeing their appropriateness.

The effects on amount recalled of instructions and cues were additive. That is, the combined effect of cues plus instructions was approximately equal to the sum of the effects individually. This suggests a distinction of functions between cues as tools and instructions as prompts for the use of an organisational strategy.

A final point worth noting is that the clustering which resulted from instructions (around 50%) was not maximal, yet recall nevertheless improved. Improvement in recall, in other words, can result from non-maximal organisation, perhaps because some of the organisation induced by general instructions may be different from that of the experimenter.

The most important finding, nevertheless, is that subnormal subjects are perfectly capable of using organisation to aid recall when they are told that this is an appropriate strategy.

In summary, Chapter 9 has indicated that there are several ways in which subjects of higher VA may be assisted, in addition to the provision of superordinate cues shown to be effective in Chapter 8. Specifically, grouped presentation (Experiment 9), the opportunity to provide one-self with grouped presentation (Experiment 10) and general instructions to organise (Experiment 11) have all been shown to result in improvement.

There are thus many reasons for supposing that it is the specific nature of the experimental task which prevents these subjects from organising randomly ordered material without help. For if many different forms of assistance are effective, it becomes less easy to attribute failure to a specific defect (e.g. inability to use a super-ordinate coding).

References

1. McCONKEY, R. and HERRIOT, P. (1973).'The role of blocked presentation in the elicitation of a categorical strategy of remembering with retarded adults.' *British Journal of Psychology* (in press).
2. GERJUOY, I.R. & SPITZ, H.H. (1966). 'Associative clustering in free recall: intellectual and developmental variables.' *American Journal of Mental Deficiency*, **70**, 918-927.
3. GERJUOY, I.R. & WINTERS, J.J. (1970). 'Subjective organisation by EMR adolescents in free recall: bi-modal presentation.' *American Journal of Mental Deficiency*, **74**, 509-516.
4. GREEN, J.M. (1972). 'The effect of general instructions and of cues on the free recall of retarded adults.' Unpublished mss.

Postscript

Subsequently, an experiment (1) was carried out aimed at investigating further the effect of grouping on inter-item associations. Sixteen unrelated items (the material used in the BRA test) were presented in a five-trial free recall procedure to 16 subjects. Their mean CA was 25.98 (SD 6.50), and mean VA 7.64 (SD 1.15). There were two conditions, grouped and random order presentation. In the grouped condition, the same four items were presented in spatially separate groups on each trial; in the random order condition, all 16 items appeared in a single un-grouped array in a different order on each trial. Results showed that there was no significant effect of grouping on amount recalled; further, there was no indication that subjects grouped together in recall items which had been grouped at presentation. These results indicate that the increased clustering and recall of categorisable material obtained as a result of grouping were not due solely to the spatial grouping of items. Rather, they suggest that grouping is reinforcing previously existing inter-item associations. Thus when subjects do not have previously established inter-item associations, grouping has no effect.

Chapter 10

Subject variables and strategy learning

a. Subject variables

It was suggested on page 44 that the research worker in subnormality has a difficult task. He has to devise theories of subnormal function which deal with as large a population as possible; and at the same time, he has to discover those parameters which define this population, distinguishing it from other populations. This section deals with two variables which have been manipulated in the present series of experiments with this latter objective.

The first is VA, as measured by the English Picture Vocabulary Test (1). Appendix 1 gives further particulars concerning the EPVT. Although there is no basic theoretical rationale for this test, it appears to give some indication of the ability to comprehend common nouns and verbs. In Experiment 7, which was described on pages 69 and 70, VA was expressly manipulated as a variable. For positive correlations had sometimes been obtained between VA and clustering in the preliminary studies (see chapter 7). This was true of non-mongoloid subjects in Experiments 1, 2 and 3. Moreover, in Experiments 5 and 6, subjects of differing VA performed differently under the same conditions (see page 66). Figure 1 (p. 71) shows that subjects of higher VA were significantly superior in terms of amount recalled in Experiment 7. Moreover, there was a significant interaction of VA with cues; although subjects of lower and higher VA did not differ significantly in their performance on the non-cued conditions, they did respond in markedly different ways to cues. Cues only increased amount recalled for subjects of higher VA. They also resulted in significantly more clustering for those subjects (see Figure 5). There was also a significant interaction of VA with trials, showing that subjects of higher VA improved their recall more over trials. Thus it appears that VA is a highly relevant variable for purposes of controlling population variance.

Although there are many anecdotal accounts of psychological differences between mongoloid and other subjects, very little evidence exists (2). One aim of the project was to explore further the possibility that mongoloid aetiology might account for some of the inter-subject variance. Accordingly, five experiments expressly manipulated mongolism as a variable. They were Experiments 1, 2, 3, 5 and 12 (3). All other experiments employed non-mongoloid subjects only. Unfortunately, little of importance emerged from Experiments 1, 2, 3 and 5. In Experiment 1, a nearly significant inferiority of mongoloid subjects in amount recalled was found; in Experiment 5, mongoloid subjects recalled just significantly less than non-mongoloid subjects. However, this inferiority might be attributable to so unimportant a feature as their poor articulation, which might force them to take longer over each item in what was a fairly limited period permitted for recall.

Experiment 12 consisted of four groups of twenty subjects each, two groups of mongoloid and two of non-mongoloid subjects of matched VA, CA, and BRA. The other variables were presence versus absence of cues, and trials. The non-mongoloid subjects were those employed as lower VA subjects in Experiment 7, and their results were therefore used in this experiment. It proved impossible to find a large enough group of higher VA mongoloid subjects.

There were no significant effects on amount recalled due either to cues or to mongolism. However, further investigation of a nearly significant mongolism x cues interaction revealed another relevant variable, that of stimulus list.

In this experiment, as well as in Experiments 7 and 11, two sets of material were used, one on each of two days balanced throughout the experimental design. While the mean rank order for ease of sorting of the two lists according to Experiment 4 did not differ significantly, list A contained two very easy, one moderate, and one very difficult category, while list B contained one very easy and three moderate categories. Various results from previous experiments had suggested that list A might in fact be slightly easier both to recall and cluster. However, in Experiment 12 there is a qualitative rather than a quantitative difference, in that mongoloid subjects who were given cues showed a just significant increase in amount recalled over non-cued subjects on list A but cues had no effect on list B (see Figure 6).

This finding is interesting not only for its indications that ease of sorting and ease of organisation are related, but also because it provides some slight evidence that mongoloid subjects could benefit from cues. A further indication that mongoloid subjects might be superior to non-mongoloid subjects in their ability to learn was provided on the second session of Experiment 12. In that session (in which no form of assistance was provided) there was a just significant

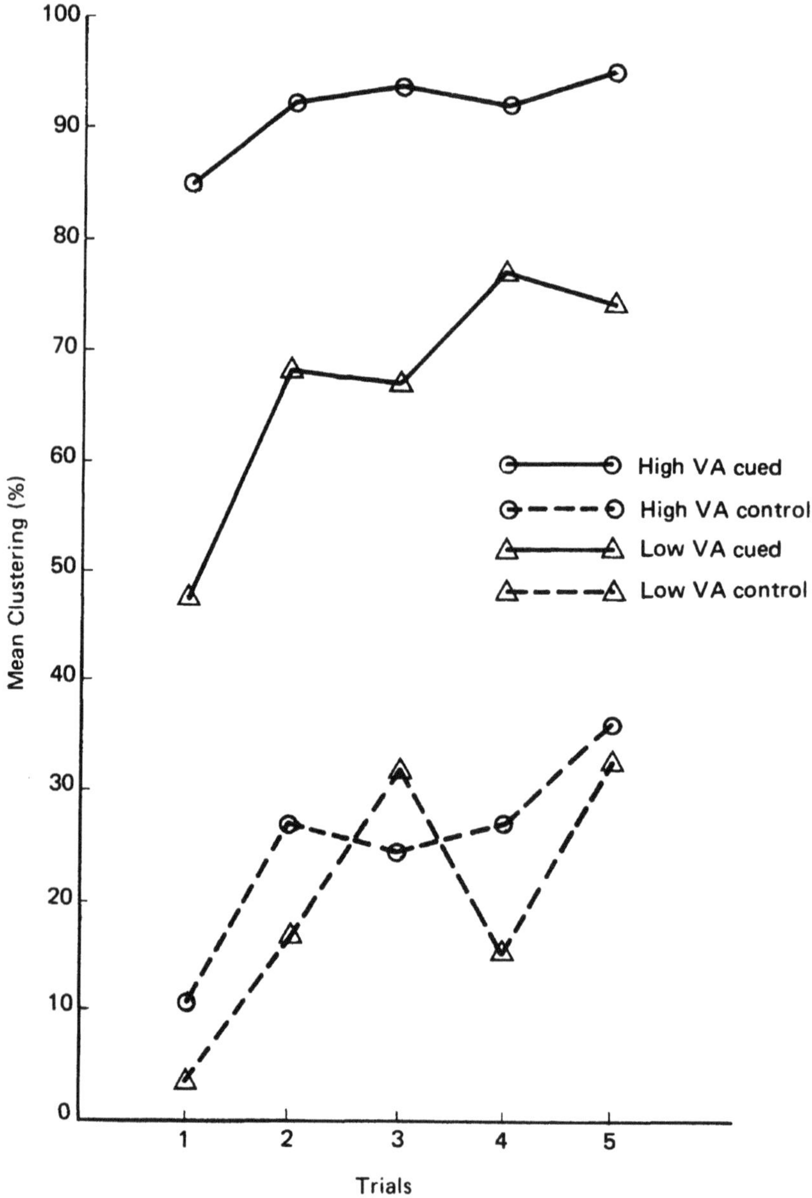

Figure 5 *Mean clustering (%) scores on five consecutive trials of subjects in Experiment 7 (20 Ss per group) Day 1.*

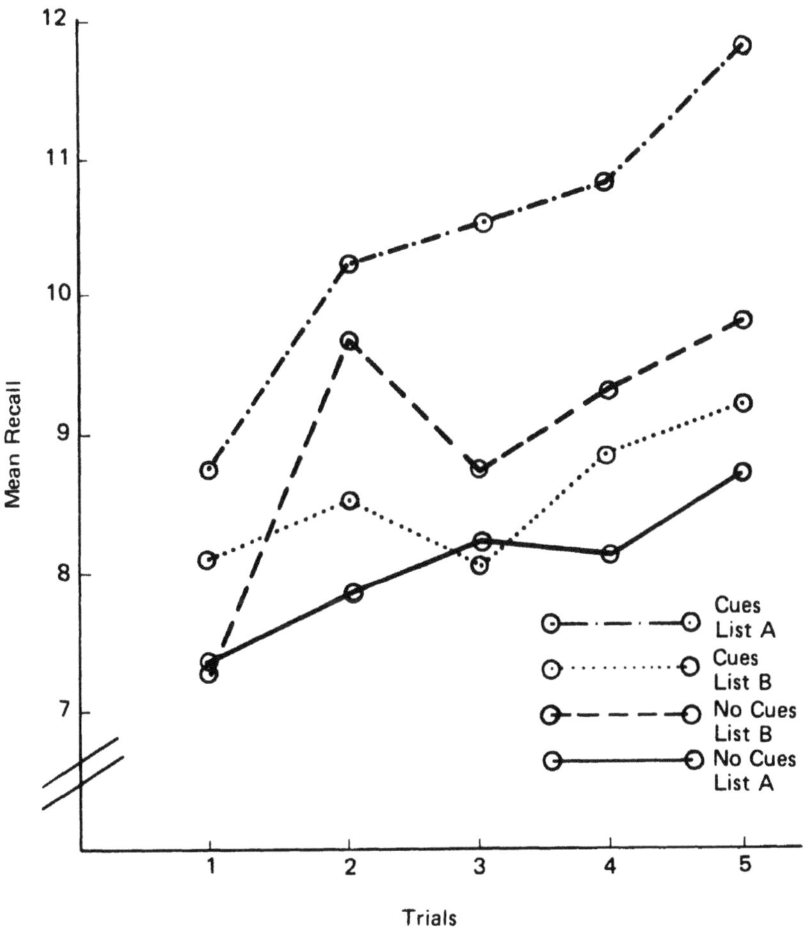

Figure 6 *Mean recall scores on five consecutive trials of mongoloid subjects in Experiment 12, with lists and cues as factors (10 Ss per group) Day 1.*

mongolism x trials interaction; mongoloid subjects improved more in terms of amount recalled over trials than did non-mongoloid subjects.

Thus, in summary, results appear to show worse overall recall performance by mongoloid subjects, but a greater capacity to benefit from assistance or exposure to the learning situation. However, the former result may be attributable to poor articulation, given a limited period for recall. The results in Experiment 12 showing mongoloids' ability to benefit from cues and exposure to the task may be due to the nature of the selection criteria. BRA was employed in an effort to control for differences in articulatory skill, but may have resulted in the selection of mongoloid subjects who could compensate for this handicap. Other research has shown that mongoloid subjects are apt to under-score on sub-tests requiring vocal expression (5, 6). This could explain why the mongoloid group were more capable of benefitting from assistance than the non-mongoloid group, even though the groups were equated for VA. In general, then, differences between mongoloid and other subjects do not need to be attributed to cognitive differences inherent in the aetiological conditions.

It must be regretfully concluded that the present series of experiments has found little evidence of secondary processes in subjects of lower VA,* be they mongoloid or not; nor has it discovered important psychological differences between mongoloid and other subjects.

b. Strategy learning

In previous chapters the facilitatory effects of several different forms of experimenter assistance have been described. The long term implications for teaching and training would, however, be considerably greater if subnormal subjects' experience of these beneficial situations could be shown to improve the way in which they dealt with similar tasks on subsequent, unassisted occasions. More important, the finding of such positive transfer would indicate that it does not require experimenter intervention for subnormal subjects to employ secondary processes for a memory task; further, it would render a deficiency hypothesis yet more untenable.

In order for this sort of transfer to occur, it is assumed for the present discussion that there are probably three basic conditions which have to be satisfied. (a) The subject has to benefit from experimenter assistance; if he fails to organise under favourable conditions, he cannot be expected to do so when no help is provided. (b) The subject has to have some sort

* But see Postscript A, page 96.

of rule which he can generalise to subsequent situations. (c) The subject must recognise that the strategy of organisation is an appropriate and worthwhile one.

Previous research on transfer of organisation is reviewed on pages 48-49. One reason for the relative failure to obtain positive transfer may be that condition (a) has not been fulfilled; improvement consequent upon experimenter intervention may not have been sufficient to permit transfer. Overlearning may be necessary (4). Another cause of failure might be that condition (b) has not been met. Subjects may not have been able to abstract a rule from a training situation which gives insufficient cues as to what the strategy is. Most of the previous transfer research employed blocked presentation as a means of training. This technique does not indicate that the generation of superordinate codings and their use for storage and retrieval is appropriate. It is also possible that condition (c) has not been met. Subjects may have abstracted a rule from the training procedure, but not perceived that the test task was appropriate for its use; they may not have noticed that the material was in principle organisable.

It was therefore predicted that the forms of experimenter assistance provided in the present series of experiments would be more likely to result in strategy learning. For these forms of intervention appeared more likely to meet the conditions specified above. Cues would indicate that superordinate codings were appropriate, while instructions to organise provided a general rule which subjects could use on subsequent occasions.

Moreover, there had been indications in previous experiments within the present series that subjects might be able to learn the strategy of organising. Improvement over sessions in degree of clustering had been observed in Experiments 5 and 6. Since different material was employed on all three sessions, this improvement is of organisation in general rather than of organisation of specific material. However, there were no indications that specific forms of experimenter assistance were causing general improvement. Experiment 7 had shown a cues x trials interaction, indicating that the provision of cues resulted in greater improvement over trials. This improvement clearly referred only to improved organisation of the same material, as did the ubiquitous improvement over trials.

It therefore seemed important to investigate further the possibility that previous failures to evidence transfer were due to a failure of the training procedures either to provide superordinate cues for storage and retrieval or to indicate the rule for the strategy of organisation. The general design of the experiments which looked for strategy learning effects (Experiments 7, 11, and 12) followed the classical transfer paradigm. On the first, training, session of the experiment, the various experimental manipulations were carried out, for example, cueing or instructions. Control groups who received no such assistance were also tested. On the second session, 24 hours later, no assistance was provided for any group in the free recall of different material. The hypothesis of positive transfer of training is supported if subjects who received assistance on session 1 perform better on session 2 than subjects who did not.

However, Experiments 7 and 12 produced no evidence whatever of positive transfer. These experiments provided cues at presentation and recall as the mode of training. The subjects were non-mongoloid of high VA, and mongoloid and non-mongoloid of low VA. However, the absence of transfer was hardly surprising in the case of the subjects of low VA, since the training procedure (cues) was in general ineffective in increasing amount recalled on the first session.

Experiment 11 (see p. 83) looked for transfer of general instructions, as well as of cues, in subjects of high VA. There were three factors, presence versus absence of instructions on session 1, presence versus absence of cues on session 1, and trials. While the only significant effect on amount recalled in session 2 was of trials, a just significant trials x instructions interaction was found for some measures of clustering (see Figure 7). This indicates that when instructions had been provided in session 1, organisation over the first two trials of session 2 was greater than when they had not. However, it was reasoned that many of the subjects in the instructions conditions may not in fact have benefited to any great extent on the first session from the instructions. With this in mind, the 20 subjects who had received instructions only were divided into the 10 who clustered most on session 1 (mean clustering score 74%) and the 10 who clustered least (mean 17%). The same division was made among subjects in the control condition (means 39% and 11% respectively). The high clusterers had also recalled more on session 1, and had scored higher on the BRA test, although there was no difference in VA between high and low clusterers. Analysis of session 2 showed that the only effect on amount recalled was of level of clustering – high clusterers recalled more than low clusterers regardless of whether or not they had received instructions. The main effect of instructions only approached significance ($p < .08$). On the other hand, there was in addition an instructions x level of clustering interaction effect on measures of clustering (see Figure 8). That is, those

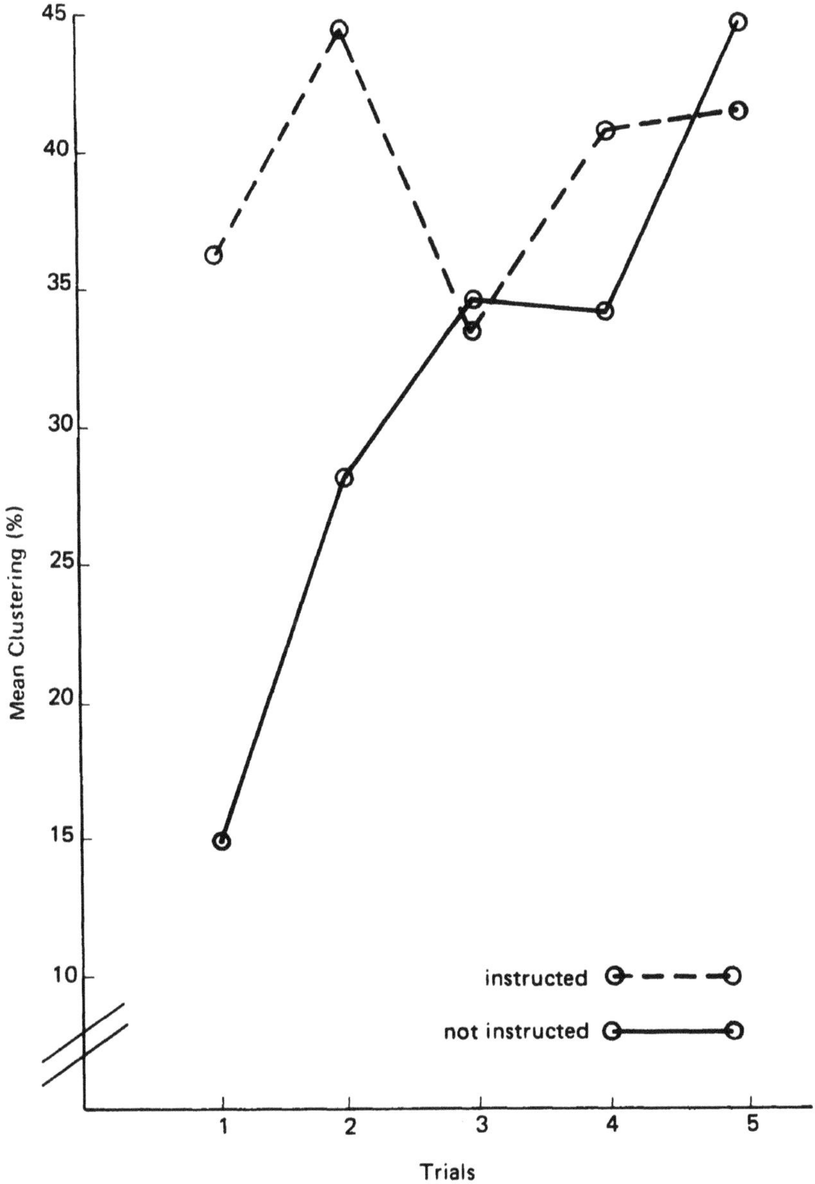

Figure 7 *Mean clustering (%) scores on five consecutive trials of subjects in Experiment 11 (40 Ss per group). Day 2.*

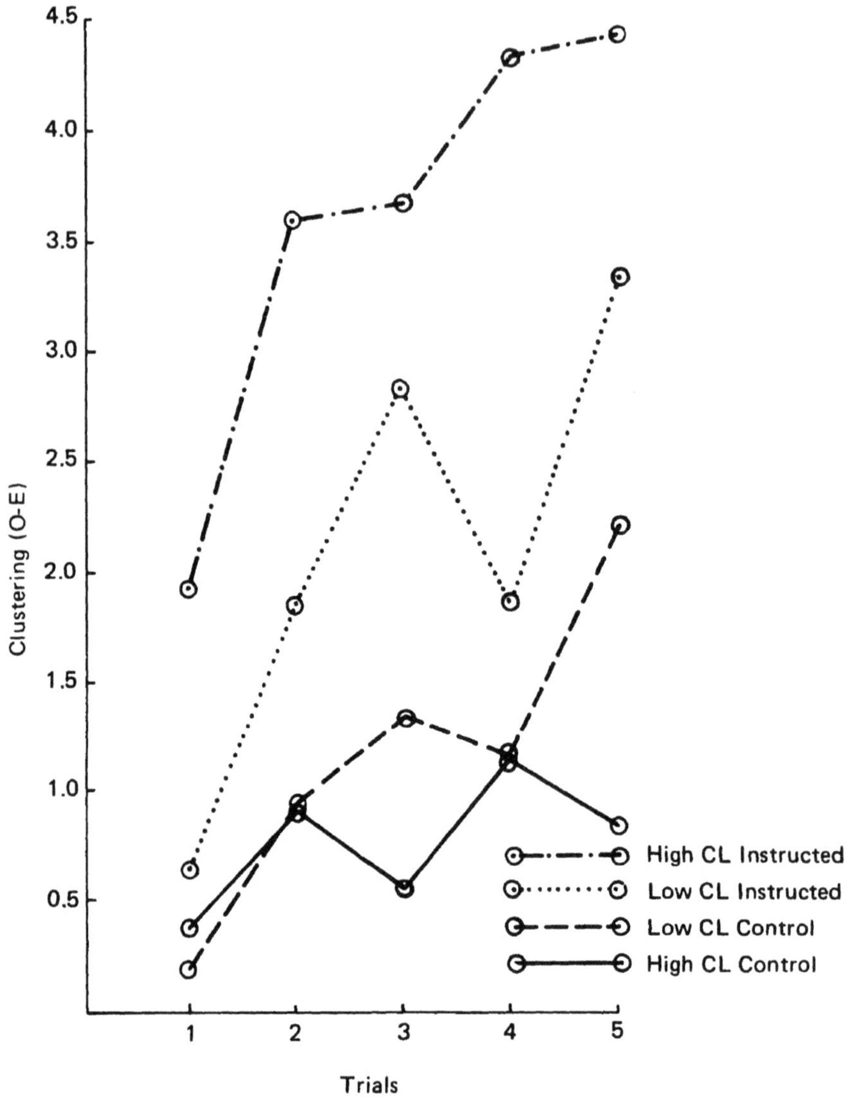

Figure 8 *Mean clustering (O-E) scores over 5 consecutive trials for instructed and control subjects on Day 2 of Experiment 11. (Subjects were divided into groups of the 10 higher and 10 lower clusterers according to their performance on Day 1).*

instructed subjects on session 1 who had clustered more than other subjects also clustered more on session 2 than did the other three groups (instructed low clusterers, control high and low clusterers).

Thus the effect of general instructions to organise shows some signs of transfer, in marked contrast to the effect of cues. The conclusion appears to be that transfer of organisation may occur in the case of subnormal individuals of higher VA when they are provided with a rule applicable to subsequent similar situations.* This transfer occurred without overlearning on the training phase. However, another possible inference is that general instructions to cluster force subjects to perform their own coding operations, and that such active performance results in the sort of learning which transfers.

In summary, the effects of instructions both on session 1 (see Chapter 9) and session 2 are of considerable importance. They imply that subjects have available all the tools required to organise their memory, but that they benefit from help in formulating a rule to assist them in a novel situation and in subsequent tasks.

References

1. BRIMER, M.A. and DUNN, L.M. (1962). *English Picture Vocabulary Test.* Bristol, Educational Evaluation Enterprises.
2. BELMONT, J. (1971). 'Medical-behavioural research in retardation.' In N.R. ELLIS (Ed.) *International Review of Research into Mental Retardation,* Vol. 5., Academic Press, New York.
3. GREEN, J.M. (1972). 'The effect of cues on the free recall of adult subnormals of different vocabulary age and aetiology.' (unpublished mss.).
4. CLARKE, A.M. and CLARKE, A.D.B. (1967). 'Learning transfer and cognitive development.' In ZUBIN, J. and JERVIS, G.A. (Eds.) *Psychopathology of Mental Development.* New York, Grune & Stratton.
5. BILOVSKI, D. and SHARE, J. (1965). 'The ITPA and Down's syndrome: an exploratory study.' *American Journal of Mental Deficiency,* **70**, 78-82.
6. HERMELIN, B. and O'CONNOR, N. (1961). 'Shape perception and reproduction in normal children and mongol and non-mongol imbeciles.' *Journal of Mental Deficiency Research,* **5**, 67-71.
7. GREEN, J.M. and STRONGE, H. (1973). 'The effect of instructions on the free recall and clustering of adult retardates of low vocabulary age.'(Unpublished mss).

* See Postscript B.

8. GREEN, J.M. (1973). 'The effect of instructions on the free recall of unrelated items by adult retardates'. (Unpublished mss).

Postscript A

A further experiment (7) was subsequently carried out which throws additional light on the performance of low VA subjects (see pp. 83 and 91). Two conditions were employed, one in which instructions only were provided, and the other in which instructions plus cues were given. The no cues and cues only conditions from Experiment 7 were included in the analysis for purposes of comparison. It will be recalled that cues alone had no effect on amount recalled for subjects of low VA in that experiment, and resulted in about 70% of maximum possible clustering. The instructions only condition showed significantly higher recall in the present experiment than the control no cues condition on the last two trials. And the instructions plus cues condition evidenced a significant overall increase in amount recalled and nearly maximal clustering. There is therefore some indication that low VA subjects may be capable of using organisational strategies, and the conclusion of page 91 needs to be modified.

Postscript B

A subsequent experiment (8) investigated further the nature of the effect of instructions upon performance. It has hitherto been argued that the major function of instructions is to direct attention to the appropriateness of an organisational strategy. However, it is possible that it may have other effects. The evidence of Experiment 11 (see page 93) showed that, for low clusterers, instructions increased amount recalled significantly, but had no effect on clustering. In the present experiment, the 16 unrelated BRA items were presented to a group of 20 high VA subjects in a five trial free recall procedure. In one condition, no instructions were given; in the other, instructions only. The instructions group recalled significantly more items than the non-instructed group on the last three trials. Since there were no categorical relations inherent in the items, it seems possible that the instructions to organise may have had an effect upon recall of items individually. Instructions, for example, may have forced subjects to pay more attention to the items. On the other hand, it is possible that subjects do apply an idiosyncratic organisation to the "unrelated" items. There were no effects of instructions on ITR, which was minimal for both groups. However, ITR may not reveal idiosyncratic organisation.

A second interesting result occurred when categorisable material was presented on a second session in which no instructions were given. Those subjects who had been instructed on the first session recalled more than those who had not, although there was no corresponding difference in clustering. This result only approached significance ($p < .1$). The session 2 recall of these subjects was not inferior to that of those subjects in Experiment 11 who had been trained on categorisable material. This suggests that the effect of instructions on session 2 performance is not due to the learning of a specifically categorical organisational strategy. When the results of this experiment were analysed together with those of the control and the instructed only conditions in Experiment 11, a significant effect of instructions upon session 2 recall was obtained.

Chapter 11

Conclusions

It was stated in Chapters 4 & 5 that it was a hazardous undertaking to draw inferences about psychological processes in children and in handicapped people. It was concluded that it is in principle impossible ever to infer that a psychological process is not available to such subjects. On the other hand, it was also maintained that care must be taken in inferring from any single performance that a process is available. For it has to be established that the performance in question can only occur as the result of the occurrence of the postulated process. Further, any performance of the sort we are interested in will require the use of other processes in addition to that in which the experimenter is interested. Free recall, for example, requires attentional and perceptual processes as well as secondary. Therefore there is considerable danger of confounding the effects of one process with those of another.

Previous research workers in the field of free recall in the subnormal have made defect inferences from their results. Gerjuoy and Winters (1) for example, (see p. 48) supposed that effects of independent variables on both amount recalled and clustering in free recall could only be evidenced with auditory presentation. Any findings which indicate that this modality-specific limitation does not apply are therefore significant; further, they indicate the fragile nature of such defect hypotheses in general, in that a single contrary instance negates them. Therefore the findings of Experiments 7, 8 and 11 that amount recalled as well as clustering could be improved by various forms of experimenter intervention when presentation is visual are of some importance.

Looked at from a positive point of view, these findings provide further evidence that secondary processes are within the repertoire of some subnormal individuals when faced with a memory task. The provision of superordinate cues at presentation and recall (Experiments 7, 8 and 11), the opportunity to actively sort items into categories (Experiment 10), and even the provision of general instructions to organise (Experiment 11) improved amount recalled in subjects of a mean VA of around 7 and 8. This evidence fulfills some of the criteria specified in chapter 6 for inferring the existence of secondary processes from performance. That is, several different types of experimental manipulation still result in the facilitation of recall.

Taken in more detail, the results suggest that different forms of assistance encourage secondary processes in different ways. For it was found that the effects of cues and of instructions were additive rather than interactive (Experiment 11). The cues may make the actual tools for the task more available to the subject, and, (particularly when provided at recall), may indicate how to operate with them. The general instructions, on the other hand, indicate than an organisational strategy is appropriate, assuming that the tools and operations are available.

Since all forms of intervention proved effective in the case of subjects of higher VA it is reasonable to assume that both the tools themselves, their operation, and the application of the strategy to appropriate tasks are within the repertoire of the handicapped individual. Each of the forms of intervention were directed at one or more of these features: the cues and the grouped presentation emphasise the tools themselves – the relations between items and the category labels for those relations; the cues at recall emphasise retrieval operations; and the general instructions stress the applicability of the organisational strategy. Thus poor spontaneous performance may be improved by help with any one of these features of secondary processes, leading to the conclusion that the processes in question are all available to the subjects of higher VA and may be elicited in many ways. However, it may be the case that while all forms of assistance indicate to a greater or lesser extent that organisation is appropriate, general instructions seem to have that function primarily. In other words, the effect of general instructions is especially important because it suggests that the tools and their operations are available and do not require any other assistance than a hint that their use is appropriate.

Indeed, it may be convenient to speak of secondary processes of memory in terms of a three-level hierarchy of strategies. In this case, it would be clear that the memory task is not relevant only to a self-contained area of psychology. Rather, it is a typical cognitively complex task, requiring the use of hierarchical processes. The hierarchy might be seen in terms of the tools or basic items at the lowest level, their operation at an intermediate level, and their application to a given task at the top level. No temporal sequence of events is implied by this hierarchical arrangement – the topmost level owes its position to its importance from the point of view of feedback. It will modify the identity of the operations and the tools to accord with the feedback information about success of the strategy. The hierarchical concept *does* imply, however, that each level is a necessary condition for the use of the others. Tools cannot be used if (a) their use is not selected as appropriate, (b) the operations required to use them are not sufficiently developed, or (c) the tools themselves do not exist. However, the primary importance of the selection of an organisational strategy has been indicated above: while all forms of assistance probably indicated that organisation was appropriate in addition to providing specific help, general instructions primarily provided that information. Therefore the positive effect of general instructions suggests that the top level of the hierarchy is, in fact, the level at which assistance is most required.

The major question is to determine how the subnormal individual may learn to select a strategy of organisation independent of the experimenter's assistance. It must be admitted that the evidence in the present series of experiments that subnormal individuals can be taught to do this is not particularly strong. For it consists of increased clustering rather than increased recall on the test session. On the other hand, it is worth noting that these results were obtained after a very short period of training and without overlearning. The possibility that subnormal individuals can learn of a general rule of this nature and subsequently apply it spontaneously merits wider exploration.

Another note of caution must be added. The evidence of secondary processes and transfer is limited to subjects of higher VA* (although these are still of lower VA than most employed in the literature). Although their performance is not markedly different to that of subjects of lower VA when no assistance is provided, they alone benefit from the assistance. This does not necessarily mean that subjects of lower VA do not have the processes available, but that they may require different types of assistance. Specifically, they probably require much more basic instruction in the tools and their use. They have to be familiar with items and their labels, and with relations between items and *their* labels; and they have to be capable of complex operations.

Two further very general points may perhaps be made in conclusion. It is possible that the results discussed here may be relevant to other cognitive tasks than the free recall task; the multiple-level hierarchy of skills seems appropriate in many situations. Second, the general methodology appropriate to subnormality research should be positive rather than negative; our task is to discover which processes need to be postulated to account for subnormals' performance, and to outline the conditions for their use.

* But see Postscript A, page 96.

Reference

1. GERJUOY, I.R. and WINTERS, J.J. (1970). 'Subjective organisation by EMR adolescents in free recall: bi-modal presentation.' *American Journal of Mental Deficiency,* **74**, 509-516.

Appendix 1

Measures of organisation

a. Introduction

The question of how to measure the degree of clustering evidenced in a recall protocol is one that lacks a simple answer. Merely to count the number of times that a word is recalled immediately after another word of the same category is inadequate for most purposes – the knowledge that a subject has given, say, three category adjacencies is of limited use without some information conerning the total number of words he recalled, the category composition of the list or the category composition of those words which he has actually recalled. Knowledge of these parameters is not so important when one wishes only to compare the degree of clustering of two subjects who have recalled the same words (e.g. the entire stimulus list) with only the order of output differing, but this is an uncommon situation. Particularly with a subnormal population where one expects quite low recall with high inter-subject variability, it is necessary to take the various parameters mentioned above into account.

However, the way in which they are to be taken account of varies with the assumptions one wishes to make. For instance, should someone who recalls only 6 items from 16, maximally clustered, score as high as someone who recalls all 16 items perfectly clustered? Or what of someone who recalls only words from one category, inevitably maximally clustered? Should he score maximally, minimally or at chance level? Do we assume that a word that has already been recalled is (a) as likely as any other to be the next word recalled ('sampling with replacement') or (b) that that word cannot occur again ('sampling without replacement')?

These are merely a selection of the problems that arise and authors of different measures have answered them, explicitly or by default, in different ways. The requirements that one has of a clustering measure and the sort of assumptions that one wants to make will depend partly on the population that one is dealing with, the nature of the material and other such variables.

In our case, working with a subnormal population, we expect to find a greater inter-subject variance and lower recall scores than with, say, a population of college students. Therefore we will be particularly concerned with how a particular measure fares under these sort of conditions. Also, we are interested in discovering relationships between clustering and recall, and in order to do this we need a measure that does not simply increase as a function of amount recalled.

Those measures that have received most of the attention since Bousfield's basic RR measure of 1953 are listed and commented on below. We have not attempted to give detailed reviews or comparisons of these measures. Such reviews have been ably accomplished by other workers in the field (1, 2, 3, 4). Rather we have attempted to give some idea of the logical and chronological development of the measures and the main reasons why each measure has been found inadequate, particularly for our purposes.

b. Measures of clustering

In describing the measures the following notation will be used:-

N = number of words recalled

n_j = number of words recalled from the jth category

O = observed clustering; i.e. the number of times that a word is followed by another word from the same category in the recall protocol under consideration.

E = the number of such category adjacencies which would be expected by chance, given the length and category composition of the recall protocol, and assuming sampling without replacement. This is given by the formula:-

$$E = \frac{\Sigma_j \, n^2{}_j}{N} - 1$$

Max = maximum number of category adjacencies possible, given the length and category composition of the recall protocol. This is given by the formula:-

$$Max = \sum_j (n_j - 1)$$

Min = minimum number of category adjacencies possible, given the length and category composition of the recall protocol. This is given as:-

$$\text{Min} = \text{zero if } N+1 \geqslant 2m$$
$$\text{Min} = 2m - N - 1 \text{ otherwise}$$

where m = the number of items of the type most numerous

Firstly we will consider Bousfield's *Ratio of Repetition* (RR) (5). This is given by the formula:-

$$RR = \frac{O}{N-1}$$

A related measure is Lambert et al's *LR* (6) given as:-

$$LR = \frac{O}{N}$$

Both of these measures, it will be observed, are attempts to express observed clustering relative to some aspect of the total number of items recalled. The LR measure however has been shown to increase significantly with list length (3) and RR, curiously, reaches its maximum value of 1 when only one category is recalled. Moreover, neither RR nor LR take any account of the category composition of the recall protocol.

Another measure which shares some, but not all, of the disadvantages of these two is given as:-

$$\text{MaxRR} = \frac{O}{\text{Max}} \quad (7)$$

This, like the preceding measures, has as a major drawback; its failure to take account of chance levels of clustering. This is an important consideration when recall protocols of widely differing lengths are being compared.

The earliest measure which attempted to account for chance was Bousfield's *Index of Repetition (IR)* (5). This is given by the formula

$$IR = \frac{cO - N - 1}{(N-1)(c-1)}$$

where c = number of categories.

To derive this formula, Bousfield took as his probability model the normal approximation to the binomial distribution where IR would be normally distributed with a mean of zero and standard deviation of one. Convenient though this is, its assumptions, particularly that of sampling with replacement, are not justified, and it has not been widely used.

However, Bousfield's subsequent formulation (8), given simply as *O–E* is probably the most widely used in the literature. Its popularity is due to its success at taking both the category composition of the recall protocol and the degree of clustering to be expected on the basis of chance into account. However, it does have a number of disadvantages. Firstly, a score of, for example, 2, tells us very little. It could have been derived from an observed clustering score of 4 and an expected of 2, or an observed of 10 and an expected of 8. We can in this case not make assumptions of equivalence between subjects with the same O–E score. The measure does not, then, satisfy the basic conditions for a parametric statistic. Secondly, O–E will only reach its maximum when every item is recalled perfectly clustered; amount recalled, in other words, sets an upper limit on amount of clustering possible. This feature may be considered desirable, since it takes into account number of categories recalled as well as order and number of items within categories. On the other hand, the authors feel that, particularly in the case of subnormal individuals, some more absolute measure which is not so closely tied to the number of items recalled is preferable.

Moreover, where it is desirable to compare groups of subjects or lists of items, this is not possible if the different groups or lists have different maximum possible O–E scores.

Three modifications of the O–E measure which allow for these requirements are as follows.

Firstly, $D = \frac{O-E}{Max-Min}$ proposed by Dalrymple-Alford (9).

(This is preferred by Dalrymple–Alford to $C = \frac{O-Min}{Max-Min}$ and also to $\frac{O-E.)}{N-1}$ However, D will only reach a maximum of 1 when E = Min.

Secondly, $\frac{O-E}{Max-E}$ proposed by Gerjuoy and Spitz (10), but enjoying greater popularity since re-expounded by Roenker et al (2) as the *Adjusted Ratio of Clustering (ARC)*. This measure has a maximum of 1 for perfect clustering irrespective of list length, and gives a score of zero for clustering at a chance level. One of the criticisms that has been made of it (3) is that a negative score below −1 can be achieved, and the distribution of the statistic is therefore skewed. While this is true the measure does have many advantages, and makes more acceptable assumptions than most. It is therefore one that we have made much use of. The form in which we have applied it is in fact that suggested by Puff (11) which yields a *percentage of maximum possible clustering*, given chance corrections. This is calculated simply as

$$\% \text{ clustering} = \frac{O - E}{Max - E} \times 100\%$$

It is this measure that we have used throughout when investigating the relationship between recall and clustering.

The third measure based on O−E is that of Hudson and Dunn (12). This measure, which will be referred to as *HD*, involves dividing O−E by the standard deviation of E, as computed by Barton and David (13). This gives a standard normal variable with chance level set at zero. It is however questionable whether the assumption of normality is valid, firstly with small N and secondly when the distribution of items is not random, i.e. when clustering is non-zero (4).

The final measure to be considered is another attempt at producing a measure of clustering which is normally distributed. This is Frankel and Cole's z score (3). It is based on the number of runs of items from the same category, rather than the number of category adjacencies. The number of runs is defined as the number of times the order of items changes from one category to another plus 1. This measure uses Wallis and Roberts' (14) formulae for the mean and variance of the number of runs. It can be shown that this measure is in fact identical with that of Hudson and Dunn. Its major shortcoming, as Colle (18) has pointed out, is that it does not provide a measure of clustering. Rather, it indicates the level of confidence with which the null hypothesis (of no clustering) can be rejected.

In general, measures of clustering are not necessarily measures of organisation. Since measures of clustering are not based on any theory of memory organisation, clustering data alone are not adequate evidence for the existence of organisational processes.

c. *Measures of subjective organisation*

The nature of subjective organisation has been described on page 10. The concept of subjective organisation concerns the consistent ordering of apparently unrelated items over trials. Measures of subjective organisation have developed in the same way as measures of clustering. At first, no account was taken of the degree of subjective organisation that would be expected to occur by chance, given a particular recall protocol. Thus scores were calculated in terms of Obtained Inter-Trial Repetitions, (OITR) where each occasion when two items occurred adjacently in the same order on successive trials was scored one.

The first attempt to allow for expected by chance inter-trial repetition (EITR) was made by Bousfield, Puff and Cowan (15). Their formula for EITR was

$$E = \frac{(h-1)(k-1)}{w(w-1)},$$

where h = number of words recalled on trial n, k = number of words recalled on trial n + 1, and w = number of words presented. However, this calculation is based on the assumption of equal availability for recall of *all* items.

Bousfield and Bousfield (8), assuming that the given recall sequence is a random sample from all possible orderings of *the recalled* items, proposed

$$\text{EITR} = \frac{c\,(c-1)}{hk}$$

where c = number of words common to both trials,
h = number of words recalled on trial n,
k = number of words recalled on trial n+1.

Both these measures, however, face the same difficulty as that reported for Bousfield and Bousfield's O–E clustering measure (see p. 105). That is, the amount recalled sets an upper limit on the OITR–EITR score possible. Efforts have been made to overcome this difficulty by the use of ratio measures. The most successful appears to be that of Puff (11), which is

$$\text{SO (subjective organisation)} = \frac{\text{O(ITR)}}{\text{C} - 1}.$$

Perfect scores can be obtained with any number of items recalled, provided that they are all ordered successively on consecutive trials, and the measure seems to be statistically independent of amount recalled.

A further drawback of the measures so far described is that they measure strictly sequential organisation. Two items, a and b, have to occur in the order ab on two consecutive trials for an OITR to be scored. Anderson and Watts (16) propose that an OITR should be scored if two items occur adjacently over trials regardless of order. The ITR measure then appears more sensitive to groupings of items rather than serial order.

One further drawback of all the measures of subjective organisation described so far is that one cannot tell whether the groupings of items remain the same over all the trials of the multi-trial task. For one OITR is scored for items ab on trials 1 and 2, another for cd on trials 3 and 4. Whether the groupings remain the same over trials or alter is not reflected in the measure. Tulving's (17) measure obviates this shortcoming, since it calculates a ratio of obtained to maximum possible over all trials, not just adjacent trials. The reader is referred to Tulving's paper for the somewhat complex calculation required.

d. Correlational comparisons

Table 4 (below) presents correlation coefficients between many of the clustering measures described in section b and amount recalled. These correlations are based on the recall performance of 54 control subjects in various of the experiments on trial 3 of the free recall task. Mean VA of these subjects was approximately 7.5. The high degree of correlation between measures suggests that, at least in the case of subnormal subjects, it is not too important which measures are employed. Face validity for the purpose in hand should be the criterion; on the other hand, it must be stressed that overall average clustering for these subjects was low (e.g. % = 20.7, z = 0.29). Secondly, the correlational analysis may not be the best means of comparison, since one would expect an overall correspondence, and the effect of special instances will be obscured. It is such instances as the omission of a complete category which are crucial in distinguishing between the measures.

References

1. SHUELL, T.J. (1969). 'Clustering and organisation in free recall.' *Psychological Bulletin*, **72**, 353-374.
2. ROENKER, D.L., THOMPSON, C.P. and BROWN, S.C. (1971). 'Comparison of measures for the estimation of clustering in free recall.' *Psychological Bulletin*, **76**, 45-48.
3. FRANKEL, F. and COLE, M. (1971). 'Measures of category clustering in free recall.' *Psychological Bulletin*, **76**, 39-44.

4. DALRYMPLE-ALFORD, E.C. (1971). 'Some further observations on the measurement of clustering in free recall.' *British Journal of Psychology*, **62**, 327-334.
5. BOUSFIELD, W.A. (1953). 'The occurrence of clustering in the recall of randomly arranged associates.' *Journal of General Psychology*, **49**, 229-240.
6. LAMBERT, W.E., IGNATOW, M. and KRAUTHAMER, M. (1968). 'Bilingual organisation in free recall.' *Journal of Verbal Learning and Verbal Behavior*, 7, 207-214.
7. BOWER, G.H., LESGOLD, A.M. and TIEMAN, D. (1969). 'Grouping operations in free recall.' *Journal of Verbal Learning and Verbal Behavior*, **8**, 481-493.
8. BOUSFIELD, A.K. and BOUSFIELD, W.A. (1966). 'Measurement of clustering and sequential constancies in repeated free recall.' *Psychological Reports*, **19**, 935-942.
9. DALRYMPLE-ALFORD, E.C. (1970). 'Some observations on the measurement of clustering in free recall.' *Psychological Bulletin*, **74**, 32-34.
10. GERJUOY, I.R. and SPITZ, H.H. (1966). 'Associative clustering in free recall: intellectual and developmental variables.' *American Journal of Mental Deficiency*, **70**, 918-927.
11. PUFF, C.R. (1970). 'An investigation of two forms of organisation in free recall.' *Journal of Verbal Learning and Verbal Behavior*, **9**, 720-724.
12. HUDSON, R.L. and DUNN, J.E. (1969). 'A major modification of the Bousfield (1966) measure of category clustering.' *Behavioural Research Methodology and Instrumentation*, **1**, 110-111.
13. BARTON, D.E. and DAVID, F.N. (1957). 'Multiple runs.' *Biometrika*, **44**, 168-178.
14. WALLIS, W.A. and ROBERTS, H.V. (1957). *Statistics: A new approach.* New York, Free Press.
15. BOUSFIELD, W.A., PUFF, C.R. and COWAN, T.M. (1964). 'The development of constancies in sequential organisation during repeated free recall.' *Journal of Verbal Learning and Verbal Behavior*, **3**, 489-495.
16. ANDERSON, R.C. and WATTS, G.H. (1969). 'Bi-directional associations in multi-trial free-recall.' *Psychonomic Science*, **15**, 288-289.
17. TULVING, E. (1962). 'Subjective organisation in free recall of "unrelated" words.' *Psychological Review*, **69**, 344-354.
18. COLLE, H.A. (1972). 'The reification of clustering'. *Journal of Verbal Learning and Verbal Behavior*, **11**, 624-633.

	Amount Recalled	O	O–E	HD	IR	Max RR	$\frac{O-E\ (\%)}{Max\ E}$	$\frac{O-Min}{Max-Min}$	$\frac{O-E}{Max-Min}$	Z
Amount recalled										
O	0.74									
O–E	0.60	0.96								
HD	0.41	0.72	0.81							
IR	0.42	0.92	0.94	0.73						
Max RR	0.14	0.73	0.82	0.70	0.92					
$\frac{O-E\ (\%)}{Max-E}$	·0.36	0.66	0.77	0.79	0.71	0.76				
$\frac{O-Min}{Max-Min}$	0.26	0.64	0.76	0.77	0.74	0.81	0.98			
$\frac{O-E}{Max-Min}$	0.38	0.70	0.81	0.82	0.75	0.78	1.00	0.98		
Z	0.41	0.72	0.81	1.00	0.73	0.70	0.79	0.77	0.82	

Table 4 *Inter-correlations among various measures of clustering for a group of retarded adults. Data derived from trial 3 of a 5 trial free recall task with random order presentation. N=54, Mean VA=7.50, List Length=16 items with 4 categories.*

Appendix 2

The English Picture Vocabulary Test

The English Picture Vocabulary Test (EPVT) (1) is an English version of the American Peabody Picture Vocabulary Test (PPVT), standardised on over 8,000 Wiltshire schoolchildren, including some who were classified ESN. A total of three tests cover the age range 3:00 to 11:11.

The actual test involves the presentation of four pictures and the child (or adult) is asked to point to a particular stimulus word from among these four with the request 'Show me which picture is . . .'. There are 40 test items in each test arranged in order of difficulty. Testing ceases when five out of eight consecutive words have been incorrectly identified. The raw score is obtained by subtracting the total number of errors from the number of the last item failed. These raw scores can be converted to a verbal age by reference to the EPVT manual, but the age so obtained will simply be the average age of normal children obtaining that score and should not be vested with any greater significance.

The chief advantage of this test for use with subnormal people is that it requires no reading, writing or speaking on the part of the individual being tested. This last is particularly important. Furthermore the instructions are very simple and are easily comprehended by the majority of subnormal people in special schools and training centres.

It is, however, like most tests, a test that should be used with caution.

Investigation of the PPVT by various workers (2, 3, 4) has shown a dubious relationship between the scores that it yields and those obtained from other tests of verbal and intellectual ability. In addition an analysis of EPVT data obtained from SSN children (5) has yielded similar findings and has also indicated that problems may arise from response bias. However, the same studies have shown both PPVT and EPVT to be tests with high reliability.

In view of these findings particular care should be exercised in drawing conclusions from EPVT scores. Although Brimer and Dunn in the introduction to the test manual say that EPVT scores 'can more generally be interpreted as measures of verbal ability', this generalisation cannot be expected to hold for a subnormal population in which the disparity between comprehension and expressive language may be high and where a measure of listening vocabulary will almost certainly over-estimate general verbal ability.

The following correlation matrix was obtained from the 160 subnormal adults who participated in Experiments 7, 11 and 12. It will be remembered that these subjects experienced various experimenter manipulations, e.g. cueing, on Day 1 of the experiment but not on Day 2. This should be borne in mind when examining the matrix.

EPVT						
0.26	BRA					
0.07	–0.12	Chronological Age				
0.52	0.45	–0.13	Day 1 Recall			
0.31	0.11	0.01	0.49	Day 1 Clustering*		
0.45	0.53	–0.13	0.74	0.23	Day 2 Recall	
0.23	0.16	–0.20	0.44	0.44	0.46	Day 2 Clustering*

*%

A similar pattern of correlations was obtained for other experiments. The relatively high correlations here between EPVT and recall coupled with the evidence from Experiment 7 that cues helped subjects with high EPVT scores but not those with low scores, provide encouragement that despite its lack of a theoretical basis the EPVT is still of value to experimenters in accounting for some inter-subject variance.

References

1. BRIMER, M.A. and DUNN, L.M. (1962). *The English Picture Vocabulary Test.* Distributed by Educational Evaluation Enterprises, Bristol.
2. BURLAND, R. and CARROLL, V.M. (1971). 'The misuse of a test of specific ability as an estimate of general ability.' *Bulletin of the British Psychological Society*, **24**, 317-318.
3. SHAW, D.J., MATTHEWS, C.G. and KLOVE, H. (1966). 'Equivalence of WISC and PPVT IQs.' *American Journal of Mental Deficiency*, **70**, 601-604.

4. CARR, D.L., BROWN, L.F. and RICE, J.A. (1967). 'The PPVT in the assessment of language deficits.' *American Journal of Mental Deficiency*, 71, 937-939.
5. TANSLEY, J. (1971). 'An investigation of EPVT validity with a subnormal population.' Hester Adrian Research Centre mss. for internal circulation.

Appendix 3

The test of basic recall ability (BRA)

This test was specifically designed for the series of experiments reported in this book in the hope of accounting for somewhat more of the variance than did EPVT and chronological age in the initial experiments.

The test involves the free recall in 80 seconds of 16 apparently unrelated items. These items are first shown as pictures to the subject via a slide projector as a 4 x 4 matrix, and he is asked to name them. This part of the test is untimed. When the tester is satisfied that the subject can name all the items, free recall instructions are given and another randomly ordered 4 x 4 matrix of the same pictures is shown for 80 seconds. Subjects are required to name each item again, starting in the top left hand corner of the matrix and going down each column. Immediately the projector has been switched off, the subject is asked to recall, and is timed from his first response. Only one trial is given. The authors recognise that some of the value of the test as a predictor has probably been forfeited because of this.

The test items, in the order that they appear on the test slide, are

Chair	Comb	Clock	Candle
Pencil	Ring	Gun	Flowers
Broom	Saw	Pipe	Spoon
Cow	Boat	Book	Kettle

An item analysis based on the recall protocols of 500 subnormal adults indicated that

(a) a very strong primacy effect was operating; chair was recalled first by 36.5% of subjects, as opposed to an expected percentage of 6.25.

(b) There was no evidence of any positional or other strategies being used.

Correlations of BRA with other variables are given in Appendix 2.

The only information that we have so far concerning the test's reliability are test-retest correlations on 31 subjects after a 5 month interval. The product-moment correlation coefficient obtained was 0.62, which is lower than one might have hoped. However, these subjects had participated in various of the experiments reported in this book in between the two tests. Their mean BRA score had risen from 6.42 to 7.87, indicating that the intervening experience had had an effect. Therefore this test-retest comparison does not seem to be a reliable test of reliability.

Author Index

Subject Index

For Product Safety Concerns and Information please contact our EU
representative GPSR@taylorandfrancis.com
Taylor & Francis Verlag GmbH, Kaufingerstraße 24, 80331 München, Germany

www.ingramcontent.com/pod-product-compliance
Ingram Content Group UK Ltd.
Pitfield, Milton Keynes, MK11 3LW, UK
UKHW011020180926
475701UK00004B/842

* 9 7 8 1 1 3 8 9 7 7 6 7 9 *